HISTORY AS ART AND AS SCIENCE

T0366691

HISTORY AS ART
AND AS SCIENCE

Twin Vistas on the Past

BY H. STUART HUGHES

The University of Chicago Press
Chicago and London

The University of Chicago Press, Chicago 60637
The University of Chicago Press, Ltd., London

Published 1975 by the University of Chicago. Midway Reprint 1975
Printed in the United States of America

International Standard Book Number: 0-226-35916-6
Library of Congress Catalog Card Number: 75-29563

Contents

Et Jehanne, la bonne Lorraine,
Qu'Anglois bruslèrent à Rouen;
Où sont-ils, Vierge souveraine? . . .
Mais où sont les neiges d'antan!

—FRANÇOIS VILLON, *Ballade des Dames du Temps jadis*

Preface

THESE ESSAYS gradually grew out of informal talks I have given over the past four years to groups of Harvard and Radcliffe students particularly concerned with the nature of historical writing. Some of them I subsequently worked into more formal shape for the Phi Beta Kappa visiting lecture program during the academic years 1961–1962 and 1962–1963. Three have contributed to the continuing interchange with my colleagues in the social sciences which I began with my article "The Historian and the Social Scientist" published in the *American Historical Review* in October 1960: Chapter I was originally part of a colloquium series at the Harvard Center for Cognitive Studies; Chapter II was delivered as a paper at the 1962 meeting of the American Anthropological Association and subsequently published in *Current Anthropology;* Chapter III, after first being presented to the psychiatric training group at the Beth Israel Hospital in Boston in early 1961, was delivered the following year as the Stimson Lecture at Goucher College. The concluding chapter has appeared in *The American Scholar.*

Such reflections lay claim neither to completeness nor to total originality. They represent an attitude, rather, which I think is steadily gaining ground in the theory and practice of historical study.

I.

What the Historian Thinks He Knows

WHEN ONE first approaches the study of history, it does not look particularly forbidding. To judge by outside appearances, it is a tranquil business, pursued through the leisurely digestion of masses of books and documents. It may demand steady work, long hours, those qualities of scholarly doggedness which the Germans lump together under the ineffable word *Sitzfleisch*. Its rewards may be slow in coming. It may seldom reveal a genius at the age of twenty. But over the long pull it seems safe and sure enough. It requires little prior preparation, no specialized vocabulary or knowledge of mathematics. At its learned gatherings, the amateur scholar finds himself quite at home. Little wonder that in undergraduate programs history figures along with English literature as the favorite study of those whose intellectual interests are still unfixed; even Henry Adams in a moment of characteristic self-denigration could refer to the "mental indolence" of his chosen pursuits.

All this, however, is rapidly changing: in the past generation the writing of history has become less invertebrate than it used to be. Philosophers have subjected its methods and assumptions to rigorous logical analysis. Historical scholarship has begun to establish firm ties with such neighboring intellectual disciplines as economics and sociology.[1] In short, after talking about the matter for more than a century, historians have finally become a rather special breed of scientists. And in so doing, they have begun to recognize that art and science are not so far apart as they used to suppose. As E. H. Carr has written: "Scientists, social scientists, and historians are all engaged in different branches of the same study: the study of man and his environment, of the effects of man on his environment and of his environment on man. The object of the study is the same: to increase man's understanding of, and mastery over, his environment."[2]

Or—to cite a scientist's view of intellectual method—"The two processes, that of science and that of art, are not very different. Both science and art form in the course of the centuries a human language by which we can speak about the more remote parts of reality, and the coherent sets of concepts as well as the different styles of art are different words or groups of words in this language."[3] Both the scientist and the artist communicate what they have understood through the language of metaphor. If a scientific hypothesis is a metaphor, so is a plastic design or a phrase of music. At the same time as metaphors they are radically incommensurate. "The elegant rationality of science and the metaphoric non-rational-

[1] I have tried to analyze these new trends in my essay "The Historian and the Social Scientist," *American Historical Reciew,* LXVI (October 1960), 20–46.

[2] *What Is History?* (New York, 1961), p. 111.

[3] Werner Heisenberg, *Physics and Philosophy: The Revolution in Modern Science* (New York, 1958), p. 109.

ity of art operate with deeply different grammars."[4] One conveys its meaning through precise structures of thought— the other by suggestion and indirection. Their procedures are complementary rather than identical. And the writing of history partakes of the nature of both. Perhaps more than in any other field of study, these two aspects of man's intellectual quest are inextricably entangled in the pursuit of knowledge about the human past.

Hence the study of history offers living proof of the complementary nature of art and of science. One might think that this would be a source of pride to historians. And I suspect that my fellow historians do take pride in the mediating character of their own discipline more frequently than they explicitly proclaim it. All too often, however, the half-scientific, half-artistic nature of their pursuits figures as a source of puzzlement and of difficulty in explaining to their colleagues in other fields what they are about. In particular, the growing affiliation of history with social science seems more of a threat than an opportunity. In the minds of historians wedded to the tradition of history as a branch of literature, the new emphasis on methodological rigor suggests the abandonment of something infinitely precious. The fear of scientific attachments may be rooted in unfortunate early experience: it may go back to college days, when a young scholar with a strongly literary bent found himself inept in the laboratory. It may reflect an aesthetic distaste for scientists as cultural barbarians with no feeling for language. It may mask a sense of inferiority: after all, scientists have no trouble in understanding what historians write, but the reverse is far from true. In any

[4] Jerome S. Bruner, *On Knowing: Essays for the Left Hand* (Cambridge, Mass., 1962), p. 74.

case, a great many historians seem to feel that if their subject
should become too scientific it would forfeit its soul—it would
lose the quality of color and adventure that first inspired them
to embark on historical studies at all.

Here I strenuously object. I have never argued—and I do
not propose to argue now—that history should strive for the
exactitude of the more precise sciences. I resist any notion
that historians should alter their characteristic vocabulary and
mode of presentation, that they should cease to think of their
subject as a branch of literature. The dilemma, I believe, is
quite false. History can become more scientific—more conscious of its assumptions and its intellectual procedures—
without losing its aesthetic quality. Indeed, an explicit recognition of history's place among the sciences may enhance the
intellectual excitement it conveys. It may add a new dimension
to the old sense of historical adventure.

It is some of these new adventures, far out on the boundaries of investigation where history as art and as science blend,
that I wish to chart in the present series of essays. And I think
I can best begin by recalling the peculiarities of historical
knowledge, the philosophical pitfalls that lie hidden under
the deceptive smoothness of historical prose.

Historians—in contrast to investigators in almost any other
field of knowledge—very seldom confront their data directly.
The literary or artistic scholar has the poem or painting before
him; the astronomer scans the heavens through a telescope;
the geologist tramps the soil he studies; the physicist or chem-
ist runs experiments in his laboratory. The mathematician and
the philosopher are abstracters from reality by definition and
do not pretend to empirical competence. The historian alone is

both wedded to empirical reality and condemned to view his subject matter at second remove. He alone must accept the word of others before he even begins to devise his account.

This, at least, is true of the conventional historiography based on records or documents—and a type of historical writing that is bound to remain in honor no matter how many experimental approaches may be tried. Of course, there is the tangible evidence of archaeological remains, and of these I shall have more to say later on. There are also one or two celebrated examples of historians who have performed a kind of laboratory experiment by reenacting episodes from the past. We may recall the learned German who checked the classical accounts of Thermopylae by staging a mock battle in a Prussian armory. More recently Samuel Eliot Morison proved the accuracy of Columbus' original log by sailing a ship himself from Spain to the West Indies. But these are the dramatic exceptions to the general rule. I think there should be many more of them, and that historians should stretch their imaginations to find new ways of coming closer to the stuff of historical experience itself. Yet no matter how hard they try, historians will seldom have the luck to find methods of proof as neat as those in the examples I have cited. (Few great battles have involved so small a number of men and have occurred in so confined and clearly delimited a space as the Spartans' defense of the pass at Thermopylae.) Most of the time, historians will continue to be thrown back on the uncontrolled evidence of written records.

Moreover, even if we were deluged with artifacts and could run retrospective experiments at will, the problem of historical knowledge would still be with us. For merely to identify something—to label it accurately or to locate it in chronological

sequence—is not to *know* it in the historian's usual meaning
of the term. Historical knowledge involves *meaning*. Most
contemporary historians follow the Italian philosopher and
historian Benedetto Croce in arguing that without an imputa-
tion of meaning historical prose is simply barren chronicle.

I shall not tarry over the multifold meanings of the word
"meaning." To do so would be to burden the argument with
an intolerable semantic overload. I shall merely do what historians are so often blamed for doing and say that in this
case the meaning of meaning will gradually emerge from context. Historians are by nature wary of precise definition; they
hate to be confined within tight terminological boundaries, and
they are ever alert to the fallacy of misplaced concreteness;
they much prefer to write ordinary words in their common-
sense usage and then let the reader little by little become aware
of how these words have subtly changed their significance
through time. For present purposes, let us say that "meaning"
is the connectedness of things.

To find meaning, then, involves understanding. In the historian's mind the problems of knowing and of understanding
are so close as to be almost identical. I suspect that this is
true of other fields of knowledge as well. Anyone who has had
some experience with free association realizes that the mind
does not identify objects in isolation—they always come into
view or into memory imbedded in a thick tissue of relatedness
and correspondence. And since history approaches closer to
everyday experience than any other branch of knowledge, it
is only natural that it should be more particularly the realm
of inextricable connectedness. What we conventionally call an
"event" in history is simply a segment of the endless web of

experience that we have torn out of context for purposes of clearer understanding.

All this has been explained in sophisticated detail by a number of contemporary analyses of historical thinking.[5] Most of these studies, however, have dealt with "micro-history"—with the problems of delimiting and understanding a succession of relatively small events. At this level, we can be rather precise about what we are doing. At the level of "macro-history," things are quite otherwise. When it comes to establishing long-range "trends," the rules of historical logic begin to give way, and the investigator is cast adrift in a sea of incommensurate possibilities. Yet this is the level on which history must be written if it is ever to approach the understanding of man's wider relationship to his environment. Here the question of historical knowledge becomes baffling in the extreme: it ends as a matter of metaphysics—and even of faith.

We can find at least four classic answers. The first—and still the basic one—came out of the German nineteenth-century school of historical writing, whose leading figure was Leopold von Ranke. This we may term the old idealist position. Ranke's most frequently quoted dictum—that he proposed to write history *"wie es eigentlich gewesen,"* "as it really was"—should not be taken quite so literally as it came to be

---

[5] For example: William Dray, *Laws and Explanation in History* (Oxford, 1957); Patrick Gardiner, *The Nature of Historical Explanation* (Oxford, 1952); H.-I. Marrou, *De la connaissance historique* (Paris, 1954); Hans Meyerhoff, editor, *The Philosophy of History in Our Time* (Garden City, N.Y., 1959); W. H. Walsh, *An Introduction to Philosophy of History* (London, 1951); Morton G. White, "Historical Explanation," *Mind,* LII (July 1943), 212–229.

by most of his successors. I do not believe Ranke was so naïve
as to think that he could produce in his writing a facsimile of
the past; like any practicing historian, he must have been
dimly aware of the role played by selection and personal
judgment in establishing his account. Yet he and his co-
workers did have a simple faith that was religious in its intensity and that was grounded in a fervent Protestantism. They
believed that if they could penetrate to the central *idea* of an
event or personality, they would have grasped its essence and
the rest would naturally follow. The old idealist position im-
plied a "most sympathetic, most flexible, and most reverent
attitude towards the great variety of original creations in the
past." It meant nothing less than a search for the "hand of
God" through a method of "intuitive approximation." For
Ranke and his disciples, the study of history was not really
analysis at all; it was *contemplation* rather—"a source of
'unspeakable sweetness and vitality.' Knowing and worship-
ping were one and the same experience."[6]

Such was the implicit epistemology of the creators of *Historismus*—the founders of the school of research that first
established history as a fully self-conscious discipline. Despite
its high-flown language, it was basically unphilosophical. It
simply took over the misty rhetoric of German idealism and
Romanticism without subjecting these terms to critical examination. And the same can be said of its enemy and successor—
nineteenth-century positivism. The characteristic positivist historian did not even lay claim to philosophical competence: he
scorned metaphysics and regarded the problem of historical

[6] Theodore H. Von Laue, *Leopold Ranke: The Formative Years*
(Princeton, N.J., 1950), pp. 43–44, 116.

knowledge as no problem at all. His goal was simply "applying to the history of Man those methods of investigation which have been found successful in other branches of knowledge"[7] —that is, in the natural sciences. Like the original idealist historians, the early positivists adopted somebody else's epistemology. They also had a faith—the faith that history could become a science, and for this, at the very least, they deserve our respect. Yet their notion of science was simple-minded and unidimensional; they absorbed from the natural scientists of their day an unquestioning confidence that the search for "causes" and "laws" was the sole and proper occupation of the up-to-date investigator. Fittingly enough, it was the natural scientists themselves who pulled the rug from under positivist historiography. The great revolution in scientific thinking at the turn of the century deprived the science-minded historians of their philosophical base—although it took some of them another generation to wake up to what had happened.

These first two answers to the problem of historical knowledge are now little more than intellectual curiosities. But each of the main nineteenth-century schools has had its twentieth-century offshoot, and idealism and positivism in their new form inevitably provide the starting point for the speculations of the philosophically inclined among contemporary historians.

The neoidealist position, whose most influential exponents were Wilhelm Dilthey in Germany and Benedetto Croce in Italy, began as an effort to ward off the threat from positivism and natural science by re-establishing the study of history as

[7] Henry Thomas Buckle, *History of Civilization in England,* new edition (London, 1891), I, 227.

an intellectual discipline with its own characteristics and procedures. The neoidealists were well aware of the philosophical inadequacies of their nineteenth-century forebears. They knew that in a science-minded age it would not suffice simply to repeat with Ranke that ultimate reality lay in "idea" or "spirit." And so they labored to refine the logic of historical discourse; they tried to chart the operations the historian's mind actually performs in putting together a coherent account of the past. Most of this work has proved of permanent value: few historians today would deny the neoidealists' central contention that historical understanding is a subjective process— a mighty effort to recall to life what is irrevocably over and done with.[8]

Yet on the central question of historical knowledge the neo-idealist answer is far from satisfactory. If the historian does not seek out causes and laws in the fashion of the natural scientist, what then does he do? The usual idealist response has been some variation on the theme provided by the German verb *"verstehen"*: the historian arrives at "inner understanding." But to a skeptical and empirically oriented Anglo-Saxon mind, this sounds like begging the question: one understands —because one understands. Perhaps the best we can do with the concept of *verstehen* is to turn to the rare variety of Frenchman who has struggled through the morass of German historical terminology and emerged with his intellect intact. "We speak of understanding," Raymond Aron explains, "when *knowledge shows a meaning which, immanent to the reality,*

---

[8] For a comparative analysis of neoidealism, see my *Consciousness and Society* (New York, 1958), Chapter 6. A useful selection from Dilthey's writings has finally appeared in English translation: *Pattern and Meaning in History,* edited by H. P. Rickman (New York, 1962).

has been or could have been thought by those who lived and realized it."[9]

Such a definition is both profoundly true and profoundly unhelpful. It suggests what every historian worthy of his trade thinks he is doing when he tries to recapture the meaning of past occurrences. It conveys the faith that sustains him in his arduous quest—the faith that by an effort of sympathetic imagination he can embrace with his own mind what the men of another time actually thought and felt. If a historian did not have some such faith, he would not have the courage to write at all; he would succumb to the depressing suspicion that history, as Voltaire put it, is no more than "tricks we play on the dead." At the same time, to define an activity of the mind as *verstehen* tells us very little about the process itself. Here the neoidealists are quite at a loss. Croce himself could come up with no better figure of speech than a "lightning flash" to convey the nature of historical understanding. And even in England, at the hands of Croce's disciple R. G. Collingwood, the doctrine acquired overtones of mysticism different perhaps but at least as intellectually troubling as those that enveloped it in Germany.

Moreover, to speak of historical understanding in terms of some kind of "re-thinking" or "re-experiencing" does not give an entirely accurate sense of what the historian is in a position to perform. He cannot summon back to life a past that is irretrievably finished. He cannot give the full sense of events as reality in the process of becoming—*because he knows the out-*

[9] Raymond Aron, *Introduction to the Philosophy of History: An Essay on the Limits of Historical Objectivity*, translated by George J. Irwin (Boston, 1961), p. 47. The original French edition of Aron's book was published in 1938.

come. By no literary device or trick of false innocence can he recapture his historical virginity; it is idle for him to pretend to an unsophistication of judgment which fools nobody. Hence the historian cannot possibly pose—as he sometimes tries to— in the guise of a contemporary of the events he describes. His actual position is far more precarious. Like Proust finally reaching the end of his search for time past, the historian is "perched" on the "vertiginous summit" of the whole long perspective of events he has tried to recapture.

From this standpoint, the study of recent history appears more difficult than the investigation of the remote past, rather than the simpler matter that it is frequently said to be. For the historian who writes about the latest events in man's experience must presuppose in his mind all that went before. And similarly, when he turns his thoughts back to these earlier eras, his understanding is colored by everything that has happened since. He knows not only the outcome but the sequels: however much he may try to divest himself of his privileged position, however much he may screen out what is not strictly relevant to his account, it is still lurking in the back of his consciousness. And such is the case even when the subsequent events are never mentioned. I was forcibly struck by this simple truth in reading over with a small group of my students two of the most influential novels coming out of the First World War. One had been published in 1928, the other exactly a decade later. Both dwelt with hatred and revulsion on the horrors of combat, both spoke from a common ideological standpoint of human solidarity transcending national frontiers. But in the second a subtle shift of emphasis had taken place; the loathing for war was still present, yet it was a loathing tempered by distance and by the sense that Europe was once more girding for conflict; it was no longer possible to write in terms of something that must never be allowed to happen again.

Thus these sequels of which the historian himself may not be consciously aware are of all types and levels of specificity. They are not only actions or events—they are also thoughts and sentiments. They form part of the endless reciprocity between present and past—between the historian and his subject matter—whose full complexity the idealist metaphor of "re-enactment" is powerless to convey.[10]

Still worse, however, is the quicksand of philosophical relativism to which the logic of subjective epistemology eventually carries us. On the outer reaches of idealist thought, the grounding for historical truth becomes spongy indeed. If the procedure known as *verstehen* can seldom be subjected to empirical check—if the very "internal" character of such understanding excludes the customary methods of scientific verification—how is it possible for us to know the truth of these insights or even to communicate them in an unambiguous fashion? How are we to assess whether one historian's judgment is better than that of another? In the end we are reduced to a flip of the coin—"You pay your money and you take your choice."

It took a full century for historical idealism to reach this pass. The problem of the relativity of individual judgments troubled Ranke scarcely at all; he had his religious faith to sustain him. Two generations later the neoidealists saw very clearly the chasm that was opening before them; they had lost the serene faith of a simpler age, and although most of them

[10] For all the foregoing, see Marrou, *De la connaissance historique*, pp. 43–46, and Carr, *What Is History?* p. 35.

still recognized the existence of something resembling a God, they were far from certain of finding the traces of his handi-work in the record of history. Yet still they clung to the frag-ments of certitude, a residual faith in some inexplicable consensus of the "spirit." No European historian of the early twentieth century was willing to throw in his hand and confess the total relativity of historical judgments. It was an American, Carl Becker, who finally had the bravery—or the sense of intellectual defeat—to affirm that "everyman" was "his own historian."

Such a verdict did not deny, of course, that there were some judgments which were more expert than others. Yet it did suggest quite clearly that on the larger questions of historical interpretation, criteria for comparative evaluation were almost totally lacking. And here the problem rested. In idealist terms, the limits of skepticism had been reached: historical thought could go no farther.

The other contemporary refurbishing of a nineteenth-cen-tury position—neopositivism—has been formulated far less explicitly than has neoidealist thought. Its adherents have been practicing historians of a severely professional bent, who have spoken more of techniques and methods than they have of the ultimate philosophical grounding of their researches. Indeed, I am not sure whether the term "neopositivist" would be ac-ceptable to them, but I can find none better. Moreover, it has the advantage of associating this most influential school of contemporary historical study with the leading twentieth-century bodies of thought in philosophy and natural science which quite consciously apply the positivist label to their own work.

In a word, the new historical positivists—and I am thinking more particularly of the contemporary French school of economic and social historians—while implicitly accepting the subjective epistemology of neoidealism, have resumed under more favorable circumstances the old positivist task of creating a science of historical study. No longer do they think of science in terms of a simple scheme of causes and laws: the natural scientists themselves would not give sanction for that. I referred earlier to the vast upheaval in scientific thinking which after the turn of the century deprived the original positivists of their intellectual justification. When the natural scientists themselves had redefined nature's laws as mere hypotheses, when they had begun to substitute relativity, plural explanations, and eventually even indeterminacy for the earlier certitudes of a consistent universe, the science-minded historians had no recourse but to follow. Some of them continued to employ the old scientific language as though nothing had happened. Most of the more sophisticated concluded with Croce that history would never be a science at all. Only a few tried to see what could be salvaged from the intellectual wreck; like the logical-positivist philosophers in Austria and England, a handful of courageous historians in France set out to discover whether there were any fixed points still remaining in the fluid universe to which relativity in natural science and relativism in historical judgment had so cruelly consigned them.

The chief of these was Marc Bloch—a medievalist and economic historian by training but one whose mind roamed at will over the whole vast terrain of historical method. Bloch found salvation from the nightmares of late idealist skepticism by changing the metaphor in which he wrote of his own profession. Where Dilthey and Croce had spoken almost exclusively

of an internal process of thought, Bloch shifted the emphasis
to what was external and tangible. He did not deny the subjective character of historical judgment. He simply drew
attention once again—and far more systematically than had
been true of his nineteenth-century forebears—to the realities
that the historian can actually see or hear or touch: archaeological remains, languages, folklore, and the like. These, he
argued, provided the fixed points on which the thought of the
historian could come to rest, and from which it could also take
a new start—much as the surveyor makes his first reading from
a metal plaque on the ground of whose accuracy of elevation
he can be fairly certain.

It is no surprise, then, to find that Bloch wrote of his
chosen endeavor as a *métier*. He viewed himself as a craftsman, not merely "re-enacting" the past in his mind, as the
classics of the idealist tradition taught, but tracing with a
technician's precision the basic processes of past eras, whether
in patterns of settlement or in the tilling of the soil. And these,
he found, since they were tangibly present—since they could
actually be confronted by the historian rather than just "re-
thought" from the dubious evidence of documents—were by
their very nature less subject to debate. "What is most profound in history," he declared, "may also be the most
certain."[11] Artifacts and the attitudes they betokened came
closer to some bedrock of history than what we conventionally
call events: mentality, technique, social and economic structure were far less likely than was a narrative sequence to suffer
concealment or deformation. And the historian who was more
a reconstructor than a narrator, Bloch argued, would be more

[11] *The Historian's Craft*, translated by Peter Putnam (New York,
1953), p. 104.

likely to reach something to which he could confidently give the name of truth.

Indeed, the very deformations of these basic evidences could serve the cause of truth. A legend may be patently absurd, a popular credence in flagrant contradiction with the data of science, but the character and direction of such distortions can often tell us more about the emotional assumptions of a given society—about its collective expectations and strivings—than any amount of direct description. Beyond that:

Physical objects are far from being the only ones which can be . . . readily apprehended at first hand. A linguistic characteristic, a point of law embodied in a text, a rite . . . are realities just as much as the flint, hewn of yore by the artisan of the stone age— realities which we ourselves apprehend and elaborate by a strictly personal effort of the intelligence. There is no need to appeal to any other human mind as an interpreter. . . . It is not true that the historian can see what goes on in his laboratory only through the eyes of another person. To be sure, he never arrives until after the experiment has been concluded. But, under favorable circumstances, the experiment leaves behind certain residues which he can see with his own eyes.[12]

Bloch did not "solve" the problem of historical knowledge. But he made it more manageable than it had previously been. When the historian of today asks himself what he thinks he knows, he can speak with a little more confidence than was possible a generation ago.

There is a theory of "truth" in historical writing which parallels the neopositivist restatement of the question of historical knowledge. Historians have been arguing for genera-

[12] *Ibid.,* p. 54.

tions over the nature of truth in their own craft. Broadly speaking, traditional positivists have advanced a "correspondence" theory—that is, they have maintained that a historical account can be considered true if it corresponds with "the facts." The usual idealist rejoinder has been a variety of "coherence" theory: the account is to be judged on the basis of its internal logic and consistency. Neither of these positions has proved very satisfactory. The correspondence theory has the advantage of down-to-earth good sense: the quixotic alone will deny the existence of "hard" data in history or dispute the contention that the historian should try to make his account conform to them. But this assurance holds good only for micro-history; at the level of the grand generalization, it is nearly impossible to say what the facts are. As for the coherence theory, it has the defect of all idealist thought in emphasizing logic and aesthetics at the expense of common sense. If the criterion of judgment is almost exclusively internal—if an account is to be accepted or rejected primarily for its artistic and philosophical elegance —then it is difficult to see where the writing of history differs from the strictly imaginative exercises of the human spirit.[13]

Here once again, as Bloch saw when he redefined the nature of his own pursuits, the way out of the philosophical fog is by reversing the usual statement of the problem. A more encouraging line of inquiry opens up if one shifts the emphasis from what is true to what is false. According to this process of reasoning, it is too much to ask of the historian that he write only what is true; for the more conscientious, such a requirement would put intolerable fetters on the creative imagination. One should demand, rather, that the historian say nothing

[13] For all the foregoing, see Walsh, *Introduction to Philosophy of History,* Chapter 4.

that he knows to be contrary to the facts. (And if this seems too modest an injunction, one has only to review a small portion of the vast literature of polemical and partisan history to realize how often it has been flouted.) On the larger issues evoked by past events, the historian can seldom be sure of what is true. But he has a pretty good idea of what is radically false. There are certain boundary stones or markers—frequently those direct evidences of which Bloch wrote—that set the limits to his imaginative flights.

This boundaries or limits theory is fully in accord with contemporary procedures in natural science and analytic philosophy. In this sense it can properly be called neopositivist. Just as in physics or semantics one can disprove something far more readily than one can establish it beyond question, so in the logic of historical discourse, one can at last get a firm footing by demonstrating which of two conflicting interpretations is patently untenable. From there, the way lies open to theoretical reconstruction. Once the historian has rejected the impossible, once he has established the limits within which his creative urge is free to wander, then he can set out with a good conscience on the boldest quests of intellectual discovery. In our own century, the natural scientists have made their great advances by throwing aside their old assumptions and striking out on new and uncharted lines of thought. The same is now beginning to be true of historians as well.

Armed thus on the one hand against intellectual naïveté and on the other against the corrosion of skepticism and self-doubt, contemporary historians are finding the courage to build structures of explanation which are both more inclusive and more logically consistent than has been conventionally true of the historian's craft. One of the exhilarating aspects of directing advanced students in today's intellectual atmosphere is the shared sense of being on the verge of great discoveries. Our students are free—and we their teachers with them—in a way that is quite new in the historical profession. When I myself began graduate studies a quarter of a century ago, the outlook appeared radically different: most of us were oppressed by the feeling that the major work had already been done—the documents had already been sifted and the canon for their interpretation established. We thought of ourselves as epigoni, working in the shadow of the great historians of the generations immediately preceding our own.

Then as the double and complementary lessons of the neo-idealists and of Marc Bloch converged upon us, we caught a breath of new hope. We saw that if we turned the conventional prism of historical vision only a little, a whole new world of possibilities would come into view. Croce taught us to see the writing of history as an exercise of creative thought; the French showed how we could ground this thought in the directly perceived evidences of a vanished past. Together they released us from bondage to a type of study that had narrowed the aim of history to the systematic exploitation of documentary materials. Both demonstrated, in language that was the more helpful for its very diversity, that the historian's major task was by no means accomplished when the contents of "the documents" had been established in scrupulous order. Indeed, that task had scarcely begun. The truly exciting problems of interpretation—whose mere existence the more unsophisticated among us had scarcely suspected—nearly all lay in the future.

I think it is quite possible that the study of history today is entering a period of rapid change and advance such as characterized the science of physics in the first three decades of the twentieth century. This advance is proceeding on a number of fronts at once. The social historians are incorporating into their thought the whole stream of speculation on class and status, and on the relation of economic activities to the cultural "superstructure," that descends from Karl Marx and Max Weber. In the fields of economic and political history alike, imaginative scholars are experimenting with applications of quantitative method and the calculus of probabilities. On the boundary where the concerns of anthropology, biology, the humanities, and psychology meet and blend, the historian is at last beginning to broaden his definitions of human motivation and of psycho-physical change.

It is with the last of these lines of advance that I shall deal in the next two essays. And then in the final two I shall turn my attention to the effect of such new interpretations on the central thread of traditional historiography—the narrative itself—and on the writing of the history of our own time.

II.

History, the Humanities,
and Anthropological Change

HISTORIANS and "humanists," when they do not watch what they are doing, are temperamentally inclined to treat the raw material of their subject as forever unchanging. They take man *as a given*—and on this unyielding structure they impose or embroider the stuff of their own disciplines, literature or art, religion or politics, as the case may be. Of course they know better. Most of them have learned something of the plasticity of human instincts and have come to distrust facile generalizations about "human nature." But they either have learned these lessons incompletely or are subject to a suspicious forgetfulness about them. They cannot hold their minds for long on the notion of man as a creature whose limits may be fixed by his physiology and the size of his brain, but whose capacities for change and adaptation within these limits offer the very subject matter of history and the humanities themselves.

Such is the paradox of so much of the contemporary study of human culture. It is as though its practitioners preferred to make a sharp separation between two realms of understanding —the physiological on the one hand, the cultural on the other.

I suspect that the humanist's old distaste for the material world has helped produce this cleavage. I would also venture that a certain doctrinaire Freudianism—a lesson the literary folk have learned too well—has unwittingly reinforced the traditional belief that instincts, and more particularly sexual instincts, never change. Perhaps the idea of a mutual interaction between humanity in the raw and its "spiritual" creations has proved too difficult to manage; scholars have grown dizzy at the thought of a human being whose slow elaboration of a cultural "superstructure" at the same time—and still more slowly—has produced side effects on his own physical and emotional make-up. For the most part, the humanists have preferred to hold the animal man steady and to confine the variables to the works of his "higher" being.

Here, then, lies a largely uncharted land—the meeting point between art and biology, and between the concerns of physical and cultural anthropology. Historians and humanists have known of it for centuries; yet most have been reluctant to venture very far inside. It is here, I think, that anthropologists— to whom the notion of cultural and physiological interaction is second nature—can serve the rest of us as guides.

For a number of years now a most rewarding dialogue between historians and cultural anthropologists has been in progress.[1] In his old age the lamented dean of American anthropologists, Alfred L. Kroeber, turned to an interest in history and to a testing of such meta-historical works of speculation as Spengler's *Decline of the West*. Almost simultaneously

[1] Much of what follows originally derives from the informal "Biology Seminar" held at the Center for Advanced Study in the Behavioral Sciences, Stanford, Calif., in the academic year 1956–1957.

Kroeber's young British admirer, Philip Bagby, was urging his
fellow historians to draw on anthropology for their basic concepts of human culture.[2] By the late 1950's a number of historians were at last ready to endorse the view that the widest
and most fruitful definition of their trade was as "retrospective
culture anthropology." I think it significant that although I
myself was at the time unaware of Bagby's work, I had come
to similar conclusions about the compatibility between the two
disciplines, and was arguing that the historian and the anthropologist shared a "permissive attitude" toward their data; that
they were "perfectly happy in the realm of imprecision and of
'intuitive' procedures"; and that they were both striving to find
the basic patterns, the symbolic expressions of thought and
emotion, that would serve to define an entire society. Beyond
that, I have contended that systematic field work on the
anthropological model offers "the best possible training-ground
for the historian whose mind is oriented toward social and
psychological synthesis."[3]

Let us grant for a moment that such views have by now become widespread among the historical profession. It is not too
difficult—it does not wrench the mind too painfully—for the
historian or the humanist to accept the notion of "living his
way" into the totality of a culture. On the contrary, his heart
may be gladdened by the new and heady sense of actuality that
accompanies this type of study. With the investigation of
physical or instinctual change it is quite otherwise. Here the
historian's spirit rebels. The notion of such change *within his-*

[2] Alfred L. Kroeber, *Style and Civilizations* (Ithaca, N.Y., 1957);
Philip Bagby, *Culture and History* (London, 1958). The historical profession has suffered a severe loss in Bagby's untimely death.

[3] "The Historian and the Social Scientist," *American Historical
Review*, LXVI (October 1960), 34, 42–43.

torical time is foreign to him. He has banished it to tens of thousands of years ago, to the realm of the physical anthropologist and to the concerns of what he calls prehistory.

Yet the historian or the humanist knows perfectly well that physical and instinctual changes *have* occurred within the confines of historical time. He constantly mentions them—but in passing or in the context of events that loom larger in his mind. It is no great discovery on my part to speak of these things. It is rather a question of bringing together the elements, the scattered evidences, of a new type of historical or humanistic study that already exists, but is not yet fully conscious of what it is about.

One way to begin is to take another look at the positivist historians of the nineteenth century. On further reflection, I think that critics like myself have frequently been unfair to this whole school. We have focused on its failures—on its crudity and overconfidence—rather than on its wider goals. We have condemned its tendency toward materialist explanations without giving it credit for the rewarding lines of investigation it was the first to explore. Take as an example a passage from Hippolyte Taine:

When we read a Greek tragedy, our first care should be to picture to ourselves the Greeks, that is, the men who lived half naked, in the gymnasia, or in the public squares, under a glowing sky, face to face with the most noble landscapes, bent on making their bodies nimble and strong, on conversing, discussing, voting, carrying on patriotic piracies, but for the rest lazy and temperate, with three urns for their furniture, two anchovies in a jar of oil for their food, waited on by slaves, so as to give them leisure to cultivate their understanding and exercise their limbs, with no desire beyond that of having the most beautiful town, the most beautiful possessions, the most beautiful ideas, the most beautiful men. . . . A language, a legislation, a catechism, is never more than an abstract thing: the complete thing is the man who acts, the man corporeal and visible, who eats, walks, fights, labours.[4]

Perhaps some words of this effusion are no longer borne out by the researches of classical scholarship. But it is wholly admirable in its concreteness—the sense it conveys of men whose feeling for their own bodies and whose relationship to the natural world were radically different from what they are for most of us today.

As a Frenchman, Taine belongs in the major stream of historians who have done more than those of any other nation to situate the historical study of man in a rich environmental context. Yet the progenitor of them all is not French but Italian— Giambattista Vico, that marvelous Neapolitan of the early eighteenth century who is at the fountainhead of nearly everything that has proved fruitful in subsequent historical study. Vico fits into no neat category. A man born out of season, he sounds now medieval and now ultramodern—at once a belated scholastic and a prophet of nineteenth- and twentieth-century social thought—just as his writings oscillate between credulity and a bold defiance of accepted intellectual practice, between provincial innocence and an emancipation of mind soaring above all established frontiers, between turgid foolishness and crisp, breath-taking insight. Ethnologist, archaeologist, linguist —anthropologists may well call Vico the first practitioner of their craft. After two and a half centuries, we historians have not yet absorbed everything we can learn from his example.

[4] *History of English Literature,* translated by H. Van Laun (Edinburgh, 1871), I, 3.

Our first lessons—those that inflamed the imaginations of Jules Michelet and the other historians of the early nineteenth century who "discovered" Vico after nearly a hundred years of neglect—concerned the tangible, intact evidences of how the men of past ages lived and thought. Vico taught us to pay attention to the still-living or visible manifestations of the past as opposed to an exclusive reliance on "the documents." In his own quaint language:

Truth is sifted from falsehood in everything that has been preserved for us through long centuries by those vulgar traditions which, since they have been preserved for so long a time and by entire peoples, must have had a public ground of truth.

The great fragments of antiquity, hitherto useless to science because they lay begrimed, broken, and scattered, shed great light when cleaned, pieced together, and restored.[5]

These precepts most of us now understand, although we often fail to act on them. And we understand them largely through the mediation of the contemporary French school of social historians—led by Marc Bloch and Lucien Febvre—whose goal was to achieve a "broader and more human history" in the tradition of Vico and Michelet. During the interwar years Bloch and Febvre labored to bring into meaningful synthesis the data of geography and economics, of sociology and psychology, and to extract from them a credible, multifaceted account of past societies; in brief, they tried to study the history of their own culture much as an anthropologist would approach the understanding of a culture foreign to him. The way

[5] *The New Science of Giambattista Vico,* translated from the third edition (1744) by Thomas Goddard Bergin and Max Harold Fisch (Anchor paperback, 1961), p. 64.

to go about it, Febvre argued, was "first to catalog in detail, then put together, . . . the mental equipment which the men of that epoch had at their disposal; by a mighty effort of scholarship, but also of imagination, to reconstruct the whole physical, intellectual, and moral universe within which each generation . . . transformed itself."[6] An unattainable goal, we may say—certainly unattainable in any final sense—but one which historians have never come closer to reaching than Bloch did in his now-classic work on feudal society.

Vico himself had doubted whether the intelligence of living men could actually embrace the sentiments of primitive humanity. "It is . . . beyond our power," he wrote, "to enter into the vast imagination of those first men, whose minds were not in the least abstract, refined, or spiritualized, because they were entirely immersed in the senses, buffeted by the passions, buried in the body."[7] Behind and beyond what the French school had learned from Vico, lay the further tormenting question of how historians could truly understand the minds of men whose physical and physiological circumstances were so radically dissimilar from their own as to constitute almost a difference of kind. Vico had said the job was "beyond our power"—but still he had tried. Historians are loath by temperament ever to grant that a problem is insoluble. Toward the end of their scholarly careers, both Bloch and Febvre turned their attention to the evidences of physical adaptation and instinctual change within the limits of historical time. Subsequently their students have pursued the problem in systematic detail. This is obviously a concern that anthropologists, historians, and humanists share: it is at the same time one of

[6] *Combats pour l'histoire* (Paris, 1953), p. 218.
[7] *New Science*, p. 76.

the most enticing and one of the most baffling of the frontiers to historical knowledge today. For here the data are invariably indirect: men have taken their bodies so for granted that they have not bothered to comment on them. To learn something of how humanity in past ages saw and heard and felt and smelled, we historians must be eternally on the alert for the casual reference, the apparently trivial clue, that will suddenly open up a whole unsuspected realm of understanding.

Three approaches, I think, will help guide us into this new territory. The first and most readily apparent is the cumulative record of technological change. The second is the scattered evidence on deformations, diseases, and the adaptations of the senses that constitute the rudiments of a psycho-physiological history. The third is language—ever the most sensitive indicator for all types of human investigation—the tangible link between body and mind, between biology and symbolic expression.

Here once again we may start with Vico—and with the great Neapolitan's single most influential dictum:

In the night of thick darkness enveloping the earliest antiquity, so remote from ourselves, there shines the eternal and never failing light of a truth beyond all question: that the world of civil society has certainly been made by men, and that its principles are therefore to be found within the modifications of our own human mind.[8]

That is, men are capable of understanding the history of human culture, *because they made it*. While God alone—the eternal creator—can comprehend the natural world *He* made,

[8] *Ibid.*, pp. 52–53.

mere men can come to know "the civil world" that was their own creation.

For the past two and a half centuries historians have been periodically forgetting Vico's teaching. Each generation has had to relearn, frequently with pain, what should have been part of its common inheritance. And this forgetfulness has not simply been because historians, as literary men, have scorned and distrusted technology and its ways. It has arisen from a basic misunderstanding both of the past and of the historical craft itself.

In other languages than our own, the verbs "to make" and "to do" are close or even identical. The mere word "fact"— the cornerstone of conventional historiography—betrays this near identity. But for most historians the concepts of what is done and of what is made exist in two different spiritual worlds. The one partakes of the autonomy of free and individual human life. The other belongs to the dead world of the material, the mechanical, the repetitive, and the anonymous. These are caricatures, of course; yet I think it undeniable that a profession which has cherished the "human" as its basic concern has almost instinctively found something "inhuman" in the processes of technology. It is curious that the very writer who did more than anyone else to restore the influence of Vico to the contemporary world of thought—Benedetto Croce—rejected technological explanations as throwing open the spiritual citadel of historiography to its positivist assailants.

What Croce—and before or after him, the whole idealist school of historians—denied was the "spiritual" character of technology. They forgot that every new device had at some time had an inventor, and that this invention was an authentic act of creation belonging to the same world of human autonomy and of the spirit which seemed to them alone worthy of the historian's attention. They lost sight of the fact that mechanical innovation, no matter how modest, was an event in the history of man's self-realization which deserved the same kind of sympathetic attention—of inner participation by the historian—as the enunciation of a new religious dogma or the promulgation of a new constitutional enactment.

Undoubtedly a further difficulty arose from the fact that technology was largely anonymous—that for most of history the technical innovators were unknown figures or collective entities who did not lend themselves to historical "re-living" as readily as statesmen, artists, or religious leaders. But surely historians—at least since Michelet—have known how to write of collectivities and of the anonymous prime movers of great perturbations. They have known that history is individual only in the sense that both its acting and its understanding are ultimately reducible to the play of a single human consciousness. Yet precisely here lies the confusion. The play of the individual consciousness —whether of past actor or of present writer—has fascinated the historian to the exclusion of nearly everything else. It has led him to forget that men have *made* their history quite literally as workers with their own hands, and that this cumulative construction has of necessity been a process more anonymous than personal.

Now what is the relevance of all this for physiological and instinctive adaptation? It is that in earlier ages—down to the nineteenth century at least—the physical equipment of Western men was more differentiated by their technical pursuits than it is today. Some (by our standards) enjoyed too little physical exercise—most of them far too much. The peasant or laborer developed enormous muscles, but he became stooped from toil;

the cobbler who sat all day—and a working day longer than ours—in a cramped position, might have spindly or atrophied legs and failing eyesight. The soldiers performed miracles of endurance: the record of forced marches in the eighteenth century is beyond dispute. Yet many of them were deformed, and would have been rejected for service out of hand by a medical examiner today. In early modern times, men's bodies themselves revealed their trades. They looked less impressive than those of contemporary men, but as specialized human machines they were perhaps more efficient. As one historian—again of the French school—has surmised, the very deformities of the body which were taken for granted then and would shock us today, were the direct result of intense and unbalanced physical exertion.[9]

When I was a boy, I was puzzled by the fact that the suits of armor I saw in museums were so small. Surely, I thought, the men of the Middle Ages were at least as big as the men I knew—indeed, they loomed in my mind as giants of prowess. How was it possible for the heroes of whose exploits I had read with delight to wedge themselves into such diminutive iron clothing? If they were really that small, how could they have wielded so dexterously the massive swords and battle-axes which the museums also displayed and which my own male relatives could lift only with awkwardness and difficulty? The paradox, of course, was only apparent. The knights and yeomen *were* tiny in stature—but they were physically tough to a degree that we can scarcely imagine today. Who among our friends and contemporaries would be capable of carrying on his back *that* weight of metal under a blazing summer sun?

[9] Charles Morazé, *La France Bourgeoise* (Paris, 1946), pp. 36–37.

In tracing the paradox of enormous strength combined with small stature and bodily deformities, I have imperceptibly passed to the second road to psycho-physical understanding— the evidence of disease, the use of the senses, the functioning of the glands. How has the human animal adapted itself within the confines of historical time? Again I shall draw my examples largely from Europe and from the late Middle Ages and early modern times—a period which has the advantages of being both well documented and close enough to us so that the disparities we find with our contemporary experience strike us more forcibly than they would in the case of a remote era or an exotic society. The cultural tradition is our own; the difference in space is negligible; the span of time is no more than half a millennium. Were we seeking a still closer and more dramatic confrontation, we could point to present-day Israel, where within a single generation the physique and mental set of the sons have become almost unrecognizable to the fathers.

I should like to begin in very general terms with the reflections of a psychiatrist who has specialized in the observation of human beings under intense stress. He is speaking of the glandular "mobilizations" that represent the organism's response to fear or anger:

With man's increasing mastery over his environment, these anticipatory mobilizations have less and less often been followed by vigorous activity. With the development of efficient food production, mastery over predators, machines for transportation, communication, and heavy work . . . the need for intensive physical activity has greatly diminshed. Moreover, even the possibility for intensive activity is sharply restricted by many circumstances of modern living—e.g., industrial and professional settings in which personal tensions cannot readily be relieved by taking action.

The net effect seems to be that the contemporary human organism frequently gets mobilized for exertion but ends up doing little or nothing—preparation for action, without action.

What difference, if any, does this make? . . . I want only to draw attention to the possibility that these stress responses may be less useful than they once were, and in some circumstances may actually be harmful. To illustrate how this evolutionary shift might work, let me briefly call attention to one clinically important problem area: atherosclerosis. The secretion of adrenal hormones under psychological stress may, in the context of many contemporary circumstances, produce a mobilization of fat without subsequent utilization. Perhaps some of the fat that used to be burned in the process of exertion now gets deposited in the intimal lining of the arteries—at least in predisposed individuals.

In this view, the susceptibility to development of atherosclerotic pathology would be increased by: (a) frequent and/or prolonged stress responses and (b) circumstances or life styles that inhibit muscular exercise. These conditions would favor a high level of fat mobilization with a low level of fat utilization. Such a formulation helps to integrate two sets of observations pertinent to incidence of atherosclerotic heart disease: both chronic psychologic stress and sedentary way of life seem to be predisposing factors. In research and clinical discussions, these factors are often set in opposition to each other. Perhaps these are two sides of the same coin that can be viewed whole in light of human evolution.[10]

The evidence forcibly suggests that an increase in heart disease has come as a direct consequence of the changed physical

[10] David A. Hamburg, "Relevance of Recent Evolutionary Changes to Human Stress Biology," mimeographed publication of the National Institute of Mental Health, 1959, pp. 11–12.

conditions of contemporary life. Perhaps the same will prove true for other diseases as well. What about cancer? Although it is difficult to judge from early medical accounts, which may actually be describing cancer under a variety of vague expressions, it seems likely that here also we find a drastic rise in the incidence of suffering within the span of very recent history—although the cause remains unknown to us. Tuberculosis offers an equally telling example: this was primarily a disease of the nineteenth century, and its ravages bear a clear relation to the unprecedented increase in crowded living and working conditions in the industrial cities, where defective hygiene was no longer compensated for, as it had been in the countryside, by the possibility of escape and restoration in the open fields. What about the massive onslaught of syphilis three centuries earlier? It takes a mighty effort of imagination to picture to ourselves the horror of men and women who found the age-old fulminations of moralists against lechery suddenly and inexplicably reinforced by a deadly physical danger.

It is not just that the relative weight of different diseases—the prime causes of death in each era—by their variations from century to century have slowly altered the definition of "normal" bodily functioning. It is also that the emotional attitude of men has changed, as their fears have fixed now on one scourge, now on another. "The plague" has vanished from Western society: it took the genius of a novelist—Albert Camus —to suggest in a parable of its reappearance the resurgence of barbarism in our own time. Most of us today are accustomed to being well fed—indeed, all too often to being excessively fed. We can scarcely appreciate what it means to live in constant fear of famine. "This obsession of death through hunger

. . . is the first and most striking mark" of men's basic attitudes at the dawn of modern times.[11] To be chronically underfed, to live on an ill-balanced cereal diet, to suffer from all sorts of diseases of malnutrition—these conditions we are well aware of from our studies of "underdeveloped" societies in the present era. What we have mostly failed to do is to apply this knowledge to an understanding of the biological and emotional make-up of our own remote ancestors.

With such terrors ever before their minds—to which we must add the fear of ghosts and goblins and supernatural beings of all kinds, plus the more realistic dangers against which we are now accustomed to take out insurance policies—it is no wonder that the Europeans of early modern times were more "passionate" than we. I mean this quite seriously. Their "humors" changed more suddenly; they spoke more rapidly; they sprang more quickly to love or to anger. As Vico said of primitive man, they were still "immersed in the senses, buffeted by the passions, buried in the body." Or, to put it more precisely, the frustration and sublimation of the instincts were not so common as they are today. The men of the sixteenth century heard and touched more readily than they saw; the sense that for us has become primary—the sense of sight, which is central to science, to all ordering and classifying and rationalizing—for them came in third rank behind the senses of the ears and hands.[12] Reading was still in its infancy: I am persuaded that the early humanists read more slowly than we do, perhaps following the words with their fingers and moving their lips, defying all the principles of remedial reading which now would relegate them without ap-

[11] Robert Mandrou, *Introduction à la France moderne: Essai de psychologie historique 1500–1640* (Paris, 1961), p. 35.
[12] *Ibid.,* pp. 69–70.

peal to the category of retarded school children. Language was still far more a matter of oral usage than of the written or the printed word: in church, in the universities, at the theater, people heard the message *and remembered it*. Their memories may well have been more effective than ours, and it is certain that they had a better capacity to hear out a complex argument or a passage of involved syntax—witness any number of sermons and the dense rhetoric of Shakespeare's plays.

And so to the third path—language. What does it mean for human instincts and emotions that the oral should predominate over the written tongue? For one thing, it means that during most of European history, language has been a protean and uncertain tool of communication, that it has been a plastic product of the mouth and ears—even of the hands—rather than something eternally fixed in the dead print of grammars and dictionaries. Until very recently, bilingualism or even tri- or quadrilingualism was the norm rather than the exception. As late as the sixteenth century in the south of France it was not uncommon for educated men to speak four varieties of the basic Romance tongue: Latin, of course, although its hold was weakening; the French of Paris, which was the language of royal administration; the old literary *langue d'oc,* now clearly in decay; and the particular patois of the local area. Each language was alive: each was struggling to supplant its rivals, and their vocabularies overlapped and "corrupted" each other in a bewildering medley of transitional expressions.

The underground struggle of competing languages—a psycho-physical struggle, if there ever was one—is difficult to document in coherent sequence. We can date approximately the moment of "victory" of one language over another. But the stages of the conquest are less clearly marked. For a long time it was thought that the language of northern France simply overwhelmed the Midi after the ruthless Albigensian crusade of the thirteenth century; subsequent studies have revealed that the process took a full three hundred years.[13] In Middle English—in the poetry of Chaucer—we have rare and precious evidence of a transitional, hybrid tongue: we can literally see and hear the French words, still recognizable as such, being grafted onto a Germanic stem. In this case, it was the language of the common people, the older inhabitants, which triumphed; at other times—as in the Western part of the Roman Empire— it was the speech of the conquering rulers which gradually won predominance. But how long the process took, and what were the decisive elements, material or emotional, that went into the victory—on these the evidence is both scanty and uncertain. Here the combined efforts of linguists and archaeologists have finally begun to clear away the confusions and mutual misunderstandings which had enveloped the whole subject.[14]

Strange mixed languages can be found in the royal records of such borderland and much fought-over states as Hungary and Naples. They suggest a situation in which an emotional attachment to one form of speech or another is ill-defined, and self-identification by language may be weak or almost nonexistent. We are so accustomed to such an identification—our linguistic ties are so firmly fixed—that it may strike us as odd that Europeans could ever have lived otherwise. But if we begin to think of language as something more sensual than intellec-

[13] *Ibid.,* pp. 87–88; Febvre, *Combats pour l'histoire,* pp. 169–181.
[14] See, for example, Hugh Hencken, *Indo-European Languages and Archeology,* American Anthropological Association, Memoir No. 84, December 1955; Mario Pei, *Voices of Man: The Meaning and Function of Language* (New York, 1962), Problems V, VII, IX, XI.

tual, something neither systematically learned nor grammatically policed, but rather taken for granted as were the senses of taste or touch, then the attitude toward language of the men of earlier centuries suddenly becomes clear to us. Words existed in the context of the tangible transactions of the day: the suitable expression rose to mind depending on whether one was talking to a priest or a royal official, a merchant or a peasant. It was of no great moment that the language varied from one conversation to another; the individual in question might be quite unconscious, as the bilingual often are today, of which among the various languages at his command he was actually speaking. It was up to the men of learning to tidy up the jumble as best they could.

Now for a concluding reflection or two on the role of language in contemporary industrial society. Once more, as at the dawn of modern times, linguistic usage is becoming fluid and pragmatic. The rules are breaking down: the firm traditions that the major European languages—more especially French and English—established in the seventeenth century are slowly dissolving. The strictures of the purists are helpless to stem the flood of neologisms and grammatical simplifications. Unquestionably this loosening of linguistic usage forms part of a wider process of psychic adaptation to altered circumstances. The three centuries in which fixed literary languages ruled supreme were the same centuries that saw the triumph of rationalism, of individualism, of capitalism, of the nation-state—of all the familiar features that mark the classic era of European world dominance. The literary prestige of the great languages was central to the whole process: one of the defining characteristics of the ruling races (as of the rare natives who received the privilege of assimilation) was their ability to speak correctly the language of administration and commerce; the rest were mocked for their bizarre accent and limited vocabulary.

Today all this is changing. The languages have remained; French and English between them account for the public speech of nearly all the new nations of Africa. But the linguistic distinction between masters and natives is narrowing. Just as those for whom English is a learned language are beginning to outnumber those born into such speech, so the question of proprietary rights is becoming unclear. Whose language is it anyway—does it belong to the majority, or to the minority of those whose ancestors spoke it more or less correctly? Perhaps the very question is losing its importance, as both claimants join in a happy fraternity of permissive usage.

I am suggesting, then, that a change in attitude toward language may form part of a vast alteration in the physical and instinctual adaptation of Western man. We are familiar with its intellectualized aspects—with the end of colonial domination and, more generally, the weakening of the institutions and practices associated with an individualistic society. Only a few commentators, however, have ventured to suggest that these political and social changes may mark a return to an earlier attitude toward the senses and the instincts. The educated man in our industrial society reads less than his grandfather and listens to music more; he is less squeamish about indulging his sensual appetites; he is probably less reflective. His body has grown larger, his posture more relaxed. His walk, his gestures subtly reflect the new character of his physical and psychological environment: we have only to revisit a film of twenty years back to be struck by oddities of manner and expression that seemed quite natural to us when we originally saw it.

And so we return to the puzzle of stress responses in our contemporary society. Modern industrialism has imposed on our bodies a curious and unprecedented rhythm. It is not so much its frenetic "pace" that has revolutionized our patterns of existence. It is rather the alternation of a dominant attitude of passivity and receptiveness with moments of feverish activity. Most of the time we merely wait our turn—watching the machines that regulate our existence carry out their prescribed tasks. Then suddenly from one moment to the next we shift to an intense concentration: the operations we perform are precise; a single mistake can mean disaster. This is the rhythm of living that takes its toll in our anxiety and stress responses. And for most of what we do, language—in its discursive or purist sense—is simply irrelevant.

Man's psycho-physical evolution today is at least as rapid as it has been in the immediate past. I suspect that like technological change, it has actually accelerated. Yet most of the time we are scarcely aware of it. I suggest that we humanists and historians begin to awaken to this particular manifestation of the facts of life.

III.

History and Psychoanalysis:
The Explanation of Motive

IN THE WRITING of history "how" and "why" are inseparable questions. In the theory and practice of psychoanalysis the
same is true. With both disciplines, the prime quest is for human motives: the historian and the analyst alike seek out the
reasons for which individuals and groups did what they did,
and in each case the method of the search is itself part of the
process of understanding. Both strive for a precise, detailed
reconstruction of the circumstances surrounding an action:
both operate on the assumption that the patience of the investigator will bring its appropriate reward—that from a rich context of experience recalled to consciousness, there will eventually
emerge the inner logic of a single decision, an "insoluble"
dilemma, or an entire human life. In history as in psychoanalysis, understanding implies the pursuit of what is hidden
or only imperfectly known: both distrust the ready explanation that springs first to mind. The connection between the two
seems obvious, but it has only recently been explicitly recognized.[1] Why have historians and analysts taken so long to see
what they have in common?

[1] Most notably by William L. Langer in "The Next Assignment,"
American Historical Review, LXIII (January 1958), 283–304, and by
Bruce Mazlish, Editor, *Psychoanalysis and History* (Englewood Cliffs,

42

A first explanation lies in the one-sided character of the two "revolutions" in historical writing that have produced our contemporary attitude toward our own craft—the creation of modern historical study in Germany by the school of Ranke, and its neoidealist restatement a century later at the hands of Dilthey and Croce.[2] Both of these movements of thought were radically subjectivist. Both viewed the historian's goal in terms of an "inner understanding" which would transcend the mere accumulation of factual data. In this sense—from our present-day vantage point—the state of mind in which the old and the new idealists approached their labors appears close to the concerns of psychology. But that is to view the matter anachronistically. At the time of the two revolutions in question, neither history nor psychology was ready for an alliance. Indeed, in the springtide of *Historismus,* psychology as a science scarcely existed. And even at the time of the second historiographic revolution, in the 1890's and the opening years of the twentieth century, psychology's most visible proponents seemed to deny everything the idealist school of historical writing held most precious. The mechanistic, naturalistic, materialist, and positivist language (in the polemics of neoidealism the terms are almost interchangeable) that characterized late-nineteenth-century psychology suggested a deadly threat to man's freedom of will and the autonomy of his spirit.

Thus the most sensitive minds among the European histori-

N.J., 1963), Hans Meyerhoff, "On Psychoanalysis as History," *Psychoanalysis and the Psychoanalytic Review,* XLIX (Summer 1962), 3–20, and Fritz Schmidl, "Psychoanalysis and History," *The Psychoanalytic Quarterly,* XXXI (1962), 532–548.

[2] For general interpretations of this double revolution, see Friedrich Meinecke, *Die Entstehung des Historismus,* 2 vols. (Munich and Berlin, 1936), and my own *Consciousness and Society* (New York, 1958), Chapter 6.

ans saw no reason to concern themselves with experimental or clinical psychology. On the contrary, they felt it imperative to defend their profession against the inroads of scientific naturalism. For by the 1870's and 1880's, the dominant positivist mentality was affecting even the writing of history. While the master was still alive, the heirs of Ranke were forgetting his religious principles and the sympathetic exercise of imagination which he believed to be the sovereign goal of the historian's art, and were restricting themselves to a documentary verification of past events: perhaps only half consciously, they were admitting the positivist enemy into the citadel of historiography itself. Indeed, it was for this reason that Dilthey found it necessary to restate the old idealist canon to take account of the progress in natural science during the previous half century, to reassert the independence of historical study in full knowledge of a new intellectual force that the original school of *Historismus* had ignored.

Dilthey himself tried to grapple with psychology of the more speculative sort. But in this openness of mind his successors among the neoidealists refused to follow him. Far from regarding such trafficking with science as an example to be imitated, they dismissed it as the pardonable aberration of an otherwise great man. Rather than picking up the helpful, if fragmentary suggestions that Dilthey had offered, they returned to the intellectual world of Goethe or Ranke—or even, as in Croce's case, to a quasi-Hegelianism. In brief, they retreated to a bald assertion that "the spirit" alone held the key to historical understanding.

What did they mean by "spirit"? What has idealism, old and new, tried to convey by a term whose ring may be exalted but whose message is far from clear? Initially we should note that the German word *Geist* has connotations which in English we render by two such distinct terms as "mind" and "soul": to us the one sounds intellectual, the other mystical and very likely religious. The first is commonly employed in science, the second only occasionally, and then with embarrassment. (I recall a conversation with a psychiatrist who objected to my use of the word "spiritual"; as soon as I redefined it as "mental," he professed himself satisfied.) In a strict sense, *Geist* or "spirit" may mean no more than the subjective aspect of human behavior: in that usage, there is nothing about it at which a man of science need cavil. But among the idealist school of historians, it has surrounded itself with an aura of lofty abstraction which has both alienated the scientists and obscured the work of history itself. As applied by idealist historiography, the concept of spiritual explanation became so vague as to be of little practical use.

It is here that a second explanation for the long delay in the alliance between history and psychoanalysis needs to be introduced—a historical explanation, like the first, deriving from the way in which Freudian psychology came into being. The intellectual world of Sigmund Freud, the bent of his education, the attitude with which he approached his labors were all rooted in the scientific positivism of the late nineteenth century. To the end of his life, Freud's basic vocabulary of explanation remained mechanistic. Similarly, just as the historians among Freud's contemporaries scorned the claims of natural science, so Freud himself manifested little direct interest in history: it was not until the latter part of his life, in the series of anthropological fantasies extending from *Totem and*

Taboo to *Moses and Monotheism,* that he began to enrich his theory with a conscious dimension of time.[3] Thus the mis-understanding was mutual. The historians knew science only in its nineteenth-century guise, and could find little relevance for their own studies in an external and formalistic psychology. The psychoanalysts similarly thought of history as a dry search for "facts" which could never explain anything really impor-tant. They had no concept of the present-day phenomenon of the eternally curious historian who with a blithe methodologi-cal agnosticism would reach out for help from all quarters—including those same late works of Freud which the analysts themselves frequently tried to explain away. From the nine-teenth century, history and psychoanalysis inherited a common canonical language: it took them until the middle of the twentieth century to realize that the fact that their masters wrote in German was only the outward sign of a much deeper intellectual compatibility.

Once the first hurdles of mutual incomprehensibility have been surmounted—once the obvious differences in vocabulary, in training, in professional approach have been confronted and understood—the most extraordinary parallels between the two disciplines spring to mind. In both cases, a certain tentative-ness and imprecision adhere to the intellectual method itself: historians, like analysts, have sustained unending reproaches from their colleagues in neighboring fields on the grounds that their explanations are impossible to verify by the usual empiri-cal criteria. And historians and analysts alike have all too often allowed themselves to be thrown on the defensive. They have apologized for their "pre-scientific" conclusions, stressing the

[3] *Consciousness and Society,* Chapter 4.

uncertain and conflicting character of their evidence rather than the imaginative boldness of their interpretations. Isolated from one another, they have separately faced the attacks of the literal-minded devotees of science. If they were to pool their intellectual resources, each would find precious reinforcement: together they could assert the validity of a method whose very lack of a conventional scientific grounding constitutes its peculiar strength.

For the historian as for the psychoanalyst, an interpretation ranks as satisfactory not by passing some formal scientific test but by conveying an inner conviction. For both, plural explanations are second nature. The former speaks of "multiple causation"; the latter finds a psychic event "overdetermined." Indeed, for both of them the word "cause" is admissible only if defined with extreme flexibility: most of the time they prefer to express their interpretations in terms more clearly suggesting the possibility of alternative ways of looking at the matter. Both deal in complex configurations, searching for a thread of inner logic that will tie together an apparent chaos of random words and actions. The analyst knows that this is what he is doing: his theoretical works proclaim it. The historian is less conscious of his own theory—indeed, he sometimes behaves as though he had no theory at all. Yet what else has the historian been doing ever since Hegel first inaugurated the quest for the guiding finger of the *Weltgeist?*

Psychoanalysis *is* history—or possibly biography. The analyst recognizes this although he seldom gives it explicit expression. What is more, his professional and moral goal is the same as that of the historian: to liberate man from the burden of the past by helping him to understand that past. Similarly the historian's classic problem—the explanation of human motives—is one for which psychoanalysis provides a fund of understanding richer than that afforded by any other discipline. And it offers it in a form peculiarly congenial to the mind of the historian: its rules of evidence and of relevance are permissive in the extreme, and it is alert to the symptomatic importance of the apparently trivial; what a less imaginative method might dismiss out of hand, the analyst (or the historian) may well put at the center of his interpretation. In this sense, history in its turn is psychoanalysis: in their study of motive the two share the conviction that everything is both relevant and random, incoherent and ordered, in the all-inclusive context of a human existence.

Where to date history has notably failed is in its explanation of the "irrational." And here again the reason lies in the deficiencies of the idealist tradition. The original goal of Ranke and the others was to correct the rationalist simplifications of Enlightenment historiography by making room for the spontaneous in human behavior: in polemic contrast with Voltaire or Gibbon, the German nineteenth-century school stressed personal individuality and development. In so doing, it was quite prepared to admit the claims of the irrational: indeed, to the extent that historical idealism coincided with the Romantic movement, the idealist historians welcomed the violence and passion of the past that would not fit into a conventional rational framework. But they had no suitable categories of thought in which to express their new understanding. For Ranke, what was individual remained "ineffable": his reverence for the unique in history withheld him from subjecting it to searching analysis. And similarly his love for the emotional richness of the past blurred his ethical perceptions.

Although a strict moralist in his personal life, Ranke was far more forgiving when it came to the sins of the great figures of earlier centuries: as Lord Acton complained, he wrote of "transactions and occurrences when it would be safe to speak of turpitude and crime."[4]

In Ranke's mind the cruelty and incoherence of the past were sublimated into wonderment at the infinite variety of God's handiwork. With his more tender-minded successors, this love became terror. I do not know exactly when the word "demonic" first entered the German historical vocabulary.[5] But certainly by the twentieth century it was firmly ensconced there. By "demonic" the Germans meant a sudden welling-up of passion—whether creative or destructive or both together—that exceeded the bounds of "normal" human behavior. Its ravages they found peculiar to their own national spirit, as opposed to the more rational tradition of the Latin and Mediterranean world. Ambiguity was of its essence. It exercised a deadly attraction that was a source both of pride and of fear. It marked the Germans off from their neighbors as a people destined to special greatness and subject to unusual temptations; what was catastrophic and what was life-giving about it teetered in uneasy balance in the Teutonic soul. Not until the advent of Hitler did such contemporary German historians as Friedrich Meinecke and Gerhard Ritter come to the regretful conclusion that the negative elements predominated and that the demonic must at all costs be purged from their spiritual tradition.

To Croce's limpid Mediterranean mind, something as vague

[4] "German Schools of History," *Historical Essays and Studies* (London, 1907), p. 355.
[5] See Note at the end of this chapter.

as this was not an acceptable historical category. For Croce, what could not be expressed in logical form was not worth saying at all: it was in this sense that he deviated from the main stream of historical idealism and revived the teaching of Hegel. The result was to dismiss whole eras of history as the realm of mere incoherence. It was characteristic of Croce and his school to favor epochs of civic tranquility and consensus, or—as in the history of the philosopher's native Naples—to follow the wavering line of intellectual, constructive achievement that alone could give logic to a succession of tragic errors in administration and statesmanship.

Thus the idealist historians recognized the irrational without knowing what to do with it. They could subsume it under the love of God; they could quake in holy terror before an inexplicable force whose echoes, muffled by dutiful lives of scholarship, resounded within their own breasts; they could extract from it the scattered elements that were capable of logical categorization. But they were unable to enfold it in the sympathetic understanding which they thought of as their supreme professional skill; they found it impossible to embrace the precise contours of behavior and emotion which remained foreign to them.

More specifically, historians of all schools have not known how to deal with contradictions. The gap between word and deed, the emotional tone that belies the overt ideal allegiance, the apparently careless phrase or gesture betraying an unrecognized intention—these have usually left historians at a loss. And this disorientation has been reinforced by the scholar's tendency to accept the message of official documents at its face value. It has been the same with the shifts and dodges of "double-think" or the sealing off of the mind into closed compartments. Historians know that these pitfalls exist: the self-observant among them are aware that they themselves sometimes react in similar fashion. But when it comes to the prime movers of history, they have been reluctant to recognize the simultaneous presence of motives that seem to be in radical opposition. As Erik Erikson has complained, "Historical dialectics refuses to acknowledge the principle that a great revolutionary's psyche may also harbor a great reactionary; but psychological dialectics must assume it to be possible, and even probable."[6]

(In this connection, I recall one of my colleagues expressing surprise at the martial enthusiasms of my young son, which struck him as in flagrant contradiction with my own involvement in the cause of peace. "But don't you see," I answered, "this is just the point." That is, the unconscious logic of understanding between my son and me was clear, if unexpressed. We had parceled out the roles—each could serve as a foil to the other—with the boy permitted to enact in all innocence what the responsible man could no longer sanction in his own behavior. A longing for harmony, a passionate advocacy of peace, may well emerge from the sublimation of deep-seated aggression. I doubt whether there has ever been a strenuous pacifist who has not been fascinated by war and violence.)

Such is the entering wedge for a psychoanalytic interpretation of motive. If the historian—like the analyst—finds conviction in the "fit" of an explanatory line of thought, so his discovery of a discrepancy, of a lack of fit, is the clue that something must be wrong with the explanation that has first sprung to mind. If he comes to recognize that an unconscious or half-conscious motive can alone bring into a clear pattern

[6] *Young Man Luther* (New York, 1958), p. 231.

the pieces of a hopelessly jumbled puzzle, the historian has reached the threshold of a psychoanalytic interpretation, whether he knows it or not. And in this context "threshold" is the proper expression. Our goal as historians is not always to *assign* a motive; frequently the exact determination of the thought and emotion that went into a specific series of actions is beyond our powers. We may prefer to suggest no more than the *preparatory* elements in the spiritual biography of a historical actor that years later will narrow his range of choice. We may simply try to find the bent of character, the thwarted emotion, the hidden *trauma* limiting his possibilities of future achievement. If we can do that, we shall already have contributed mightily to historical understanding, even though our formulation of the motive that finally triggered a crucial decision may remain forever subject to debate.

A few examples from my own teaching experience may serve to illuminate what I mean by locating the preparatory elements in an individual's emotional make-up. I first recall my own excitement—and I trust that of my students—when one of them in seminar accidentally stumbled on the psychological understanding that was eluding him. The seminar report had begun rather tentatively: soon the student was deep in quicksand, and by the end of half an hour he was foundering in a mass of contradictions. Finally he confessed in some desperation that he could make no sense of his protagonist's behavior. The figure in question was a war hero and an expert on armament. At the same time he was a man of the Left, he hated war, and he hoped that his country could avoid having to fight another one. In view of his previous experience and competence, he had been appointed to a ministry directing one of the technical branches of the military establishment. Into this work he threw himself with zeal; he labored conscientiously to develop arms of the highest proficiency. Yet somehow nothing got done—he bogged down in fussy detail, and little progressed beyond the stage of the drawing board and the prototype. Meantime his enemies were beginning to accuse him of administrative sabotage and even of treason.

My student—who was convinced of his subject's personal integrity—was at a loss for an explanation. As he wrestled with his problem and finally confessed his inability to solve it, the solution lay right before him—like justice in Plato's *Republic,* kicking around our feet unnoticed. For the student had quite unwittingly run up against a classic case of inner conflict. His protagonist's technical and military pride was locked in hidden combat with his leftist and pacifist leanings. The minister could not permit himself to recognize this openly— he could not allow the struggle that was tearing him apart to rise to full consciousness. To do so would have been to betray one or the other, either his ideological allegiance or his professional and administrative responsibility. So the only way he was able to settle the issue was by letting his unconscious do the work; his hidden preference eventually revealed itself through the peculiarly insidious device of sabotage masking as an ultrascrupulous performance of duty.

Few cases are as neat as this. Yet it suggests a whole approach to the study of one particular form of incoherent behavior—that is, the contradictions arising from a simultaneous allegiance to two incompatible ideals or ideologies, one of which has not yet reached full consciousness. I think this is especially true of the type of social and cultural change that is felt as devastating to the emotional life of the community.

Contradiction and conflict are inevitable when the prevalent modes of expression fail to keep pace—as they usually do— with an unfamiliar social reality. In such cases ritual is often the only recourse: traditional words and gestures give comfort when the external features of life have become charged with a threat which is all the more terrible for being only half understood. I think that one of the great strengths of Johan Huizinga's beautiful book, *The Waning of the Middle Ages,* is the way it demonstrates how in the fourteenth and fifteenth centuries the elaboration of protocol and of ritualistic behavior served as a reassurance against unbearable anxiety: here on a wider scale we find the same kind of compulsive meticulousness that we observed just now in an isolated individual's response to ideological distress.

I recall another student—this time at the Ph.D. dissertation stage—who underwent a crisis of self-doubt in the course of his research. His subject was again biographical: a historian and literary figure, not himself of first rank, but a close observer and even an intimate of the great. Having outlived nearly all his contemporaries, he had leisure for reflection on his own past and was flattered when my student wrote that he was already engaged in tracing his career and influence. Soon the two became personally acquainted: as their talks progressed and the student ransacked his subject's personal papers, he gradually came to feel that he understood the "old boy" pretty well. But what he found disconcerted him. Here once more the problem arose from conflicting ideological statements: as another contemporary put it, the old littérateur was "a man of the Right who thought himself to be of the Left" (or was it the other way around?). My student had penetrated to the earliest evidences of these contradictions: he had discovered that the familiar revolt against parental ideals had in this case been transmuted into close identification with the father's cultural values; the result had been a lack of self-confidence and a tendency to dilettantism—perhaps even a deficiency in what the French call *sérieux*. The psychological pieces fitted together in the student's mind. Yet the conclusion seemed too trivial to stand muster as a creditable research performance.

Actually the conclusion was not trivial at all, and the final results were admirable. My student's puzzlement derived from his own scruples about the apparent simplicity of his findings —a common complaint in an academic tradition which likes to see a few drops of sweat still adhering to a job well done. What he had discovered had been neither easy nor obvious. It simply appeared so once he had successfully carried it through: now that he had finally understood his problem, he could not imagine his readers or his professors failing to reach the same results with ridiculous ease. (I am reminded of a friend who on the completion of his own psychoanalysis wondered whether it had really been necessary to go through "all that" in order to arrive at some rather platitudinous convictions about his personal behavior.) In both instances, the investigators forgot that what in the end looked like platitude at the start had been a great riddle. It appeared simple *only because they had understood it*—indeed, its very simplicity was a sign that, *from their standpoint*, they had understood it correctly. One of the most grievous deceptions encountered in teaching or writing is the sense that the very theme of one's work is dissolving into nothingness just at the moment in which one is beginning to encompass it. As the analyst well knows, it is often harder to deal with triumph than with disaster.

In the case of the elderly man of letters, there was much in
the student's own origins and cultural associations which could
help in establishing mutual comprehension. There was a good
fit between the subject and the mind approaching it. This, I
think, is a criterion often forgotten in the selection of a Ph.D.
topic. Unless there is some emotional tie, some elective affinity linking the student to his subject of study, the results
will be pedantic and perfunctory; the writer will succumb to
the tedium of which those in graduate school so often and so
justly complain. Croce and his fellow idealists recognized the
importance of "spiritual" commitment to a specific scholarly
endeavor: it was at the basis of their celebrated distinction
between true history and "chronicle." But they were not
equipped to handle the trickier problem of an emotional pull
that has not yet reached consciousness. A case of religious
doubt, for instance, may become manifest only when a student
finds himself drawn to the historical investigation of co-
religionists who in their own time hovered on the edge of
heresy, and the very study of the heterodox may prove to be
the means of resolving the unsuspected crisis of faith.

A final example of the sort of historical research I have in
mind is more strictly psychoanalytic. It is an account of the
early career of the Nazi propaganda chief, Joseph Goebbels,
drawing heavily on the subject's own youthful literary efforts.[7]
The author's psychoanalytic competence is almost professional: it is quite apparent that he knows intimately whereof
he speaks. And it is significant that his interpretation does not
fasten on his protagonist's obvious handicap—a clubfoot—

[7] Richard MacMasters Hunt, *Joseph Goebbels: A Study of the Formation of his National-Socialist Consciousness* (unpublished dissertation:
Harvard University, 1960).

which a cruder psychological study might have made the showpiece of a melodramatic story. It focuses rather on Goebbels' uncertain, marginal class position and on the loss of his ancestral Catholic faith. The result, the author finds, was an agonizing questioning of personal identity and the need to give himself over completely to a loved savior (Goebbels' vocabulary, as in the case of so many other professed atheists, remained religious and Christian), a redeemer who in the end proved to be Adolf Hitler.

In broader terms, this study draws attention to the fact that by far the greater part of the high-ranking Nazi leaders, like Goebbels and Hitler himself, came from originally Catholic families who had fallen away from the faith of their fathers. Here once more it is so simple a matter to make the count that in doing so one may be accused of underlining the obvious. But in fact the historians of the period have done little with the evidence that lay ready to hand: few have seen the importance of religion—and more particularly the sense of a religious void which cried out for a substitute belief—in the formation of an authoritarian ideology. Indeed, this account of Goebbels' youth sketches an entire configuration of personal motives that to date has been relatively unexplored. In common with Erikson's book on the young Luther—whose example it follows—the work attempts to untangle an emotional and social interlocking which is more elusive than the economic-religious configuration defined by Weber two generations ago. It suggests that the simultaneous and reinforcing pressures of thwarted sexual impulse, religious yearning, and class uncertainty together produce an explosive complex—and a complex characteristic of the twentieth century. From such an interpretation of the emotional history of a single individual, we may derive a more general understanding of our own era as an age of desperate search for identity.

Up to now I have spoken almost exclusively of personal biography. It may be objected that psychoanalytic interpretations have long since been established in this field, and that I have been trying to force a door which already stands open. It is quite true that in the past two or three decades the psychoanalytic biography has become a recognized historical and literary genre. But it is by no means sure that the results have been fortunate: far too many efforts of this sort are over-ambitious and betray the hand of the amateur in stretching a few scraps of emotional data far beyond their interpretative capacities. Many of them read like poor imitations of Freud's *Leonardo da Vinci*—itself a tour de force exploiting scanty evidence to the full, but scarcely a model for lesser men to follow.

What is chiefly wrong with the conventional psychoanalytic biography is its crude unilateralism. It suggests a one-to-one relationship, arguing that the protagonist did this or that *because* of some painful experience in early childhood. The explanation comes out too pat, and the trauma in question is almost invariably viewed as a handicap and no more. It took a literary critic—Edmund Wilson—to give us "the conception of superior strength as inseparable from disability, . . . the idea that genius and disease . . . may be inextricably bound up together."[8] And subsequently Erikson has deepened the same insight in his depiction of Luther's struggles with his early scruples, his triumph over his emotional vulnerability in

[8] *The Wound and the Bow* (Cambridge, Mass., 1941), pp. 287, 289.

his middle period, and the return of psychopathic symptoms in the authoritarian behavior of his last years.

Yet the image of Luther that abides with us is of a man who has transformed his weakness into spiritual power and the gift of speaking directly to the emotional needs of his fellow men. For this understanding we historians are greatly in Erikson's debt. We are likewise indebted to him for his stress on the years of adolescence and early manhood—roughly from the age of fifteen to thirty—as decisive in the careers of the great men of the past. Here again Erikson has corrected the one-sidedness of the more usual psychoanalytic biography. In line with the emphasis on personal identity and the ego in post-Freudian analytic practice, he has shifted the focus from childhood trauma to youthful struggle for self-definition. Such an approach is far more congenial to the historian's mind than the earlier (and almost exclusive) stress on the first six or seven years of life. Almost by definition, history prefers to deal with epochs of full consciousness, whether in the evolution of peoples or in the career of an individual. Moreover, an emphasis on adolescence and early manhood facilitates the historian's task. Reliable evidence on childhood is usually scanty, even in the lives of very prominent men, and if the biographer is told that this alone is decisive, he is in effect forced to choose between equally unpalatable alternatives. He may either renounce a psychoanalytic interpretation entirely, or make a highly risky extrapolation, in which his lack of clinical experience is almost sure to lead him astray. In contrast, the years from fifteen to thirty are often well documented—the problem has simply been that historians have not quite known what to do with the data at their disposal.

If we historians, then, accept these two working assumptions—that the individual trauma itself may well be the spur to major thought and action, and that the years of early maturity are decisive in the establishment of permanent ideal allegiances—we shall be in a better position to go beyond biography to a more general analysis of leading groups in society. In the course of setting the individual psychoanalytic study on firmer ground, we shall have found interpretative principles capable of wider application. I have already suggested this in referring to the fact that Goebbels' apostasy from Catholicism was an experience common to the higher Nazi leadership. One of the virtues of the psychoanalytic approach is the possibility it offers of simultaneously extending and testing a hypothesis about the motives of a single historical figure by seeing how it fits other men placed in similar circumstances.

Arnold J. Toynbee—with his customary talent for coining historical terminology that is awkward and at the same time manages to stick—has referred to the emergence in the past generation of a new type of history which he calls "prosopographical," that is, a historical approach which personifies abstractions: churches, parliaments, and the like. He is particularly impressed with the study of institutions through close biographical analysis of the elites that have controlled them. Such an approach, he maintains, can bridge "the gap between human beings and institutions, the most favorable situations" being "those in which a relatively small minority of the participants in a society, constituting a more or less strictly closed social circle, control between them one or more of their society's more important institutions, or even the society's whole life."[9] Where Toynbee finds this method most successful is in

[9] *Reconsiderations, A Study of History*, vol. XII, (London, 1961), p. 122.

the study of well-defined oligarchies such as those which ruled eighteenth-century England or late republican Rome. He is less sure that the "prosopographical" technique will work in situations of broad democratic participation in public affairs.

It is precisely here that psychoanalytic evidence is relevant. I quite agree with Toynbee that one of the major problems historians face is bridging the gap between human beings and institutions—finding the link between personal and group experience. And I also grant that psychoanalytic interpretations to date have dealt more successfully with individual historical figures than with the lives of communities. Or—at the other end of the scale—they have offered imaginative suggestions for understanding a mass emotional phenomenon such as the pervading sense of despair following the Black Death, or a widely ramifying aesthetic movement such as Romanticism. In contrast, the middle level—interpretations of the thought and action of groups small enough to be clearly identified and studied in some detail—has mostly been lacking. There has been nothing quite corresponding to the statistically based analyses of oligarchies to which Toynbee refers.

More closely considered, however, the psychoanalytic approach offers advantages for this type of study which a conventional statistical assessment cannot match. The latter almost necessarily rests on *external* evidence—on common criteria that are readily apparent and hence easily compared, such as membership in an elite. A psychoanalytic interpretation may also use external criteria in defining its problem group: high-ranking Nazi leadership is a case in point. But it will go beyond this to inquire about common *emotional experience*—about shared anxieties and aspirations which may be all the more decisive for being only partially conscious. And it will find that experiences such as these cut across the conventional delimitations of class or elite groups. Thus they point to a way of understanding motivations in a democratic or quasi-democratic community in which elites are ill-defined.

I suggest that historians might experiment with drawing up rosters of personalities from specified periods for whom biographical evidence is sufficient and in whom they suspect the existence of an emotional common denominator; by subjecting these biographies to detailed comparative scrutiny they may arrive at valid generalizations about the deep-seated fears and ideal strivings of the era or eras in question. (I mean "valid" in the sense that their interpretations rest on the experience of verifiable men and women, rather than being impressionistic constructions which skeptical colleagues can so easily dismiss as figments of the imagination.) I have in mind the application to past ages of comparative biographical techniques such as Robert Jay Lifton has devised for assessing the experience of the victims of thought control in Communist China.[10] Other examples will doubtless occur to any historian who has grappled with the agonizing difficulty of expressing the "spirit" of an era in terms specific enough to carry conviction to his readers.

Here we arrive at the nub of our whole problem. If psychoanalysis can help history to cope with its supreme difficulty—the motivation of the great historical actors of the past—it can also suggest a way of linking the emotional experience of the individual to that of the wider group. Although this latter contribution has so far produced fewer results than has the isolated biographical study, its major lines of inquiry are beginning to be defined. The pioneer work of men like Erikson and

[10] *Thought Reform and the Psychology of Totalism* (New York, 1961).

Lifton has given us new guideposts for pursuing a very old task. In particular, it has shown us that we historians have been right all along in stressing individuality and the unique quality of personal experience. But it turns out that we have been right for rather different reasons from those alleged by the idealist school. It is not that there is something "ineffable" about the individual—it is not that human personality is too sacred a matter to be meddled with by the scientific and the profane: with human motives, as with anything else, systematic (or, if one will, scientific) generalization is indispensable to understanding and communication. It is rather that the individual consciousness is our final datum, the bedrock of what we know. The major tradition of modern Western philosophy—whether springing from Locke or from Descartes —has always known this; it has asserted again and again that we must go back to the individual's own mind (and ultimately to that of the investigator himself) in order to find ourselves on solid ground.

This conviction the historian shares with the psychoanalyst. Neither is metaphysically inclined. Both try to keep up the pretense that they can go about their professional labors without inquiring too deeply into ultimate philosophical matters. Yet in fact they have a common metaphysic. Both believe in the radical subjectivity of human understanding. At the same time—and for similar reasons—both yearn to escape from the prison of the individual consciousness, or rather, to break out of the double confinement of the investigator's mind and of that other mind (whether of historical actor or analysand) with which he is trying to bring his own consciousness into sympathetic response. Both know that the way to individual understanding lies through the almost imperceptible altera-

tions that the historian's or the psychoanalyst's mind itself
undergoes in the course of groping its way toward its subject.
And both are beginning to realize that the same holds for the
effort to escape from the conventional tête-à-tête of two isolated psyches: they have found that the study of the individual
is notably enriched by its association with one directed toward
a wider group. Together the historian and the psychoanalyst
have discovered the overriding importance of locating and exploiting such a group; they have finally realized that the individual can be understood in his full cultural context only if
his spiritual biography is viewed in relation to the lives of
others with whom he has deep-seated emotional affinities.

So in history as in psychoanalysis we may conclude that the
path to the fuller understanding of the individual lies through
the group—and vice versa. In both cases, the explanation of
motive runs from the single human being to others comparable
to him, and then back to the individual once more, as the
ramifying thought and action of both are gradually illumi-
nated. This reciprocal method is the ultimate concern that
history and psychoanalysis share. In both cases, its systematic
development has barely begun.

The individual consciousness is likewise the training ground
of the two professions. In the one case, this is fully recognized:
a psychoanalyst's experience of his own analysis forms a central
element in his education. With the young historian, precedent
and protocol are less clear: in his graduate training there is
no conscious effort to encourage or to direct the student's sympathetic imagination which corresponds to the discipline in
the handling of documents that he receives in seminar. I think
this is a grave error. The exercise of "intuition" is at least as

important to the historian as his sureness of touch in documentary interpretation. By now it must be apparent that a major polemical purpose of these essays is to stimulate the release of historical study from its bondage to libraries and documents. I have mentioned field work as one way of letting in fresh air. Some variety of psychoanalytic training would be another.

I am far from clear as to what form this training might best take. A full psychoanalysis would certainly be too long and expensive for most Ph.D. candidates—and some would be temperamentally unfitted for it. In a few cases, however, it might be precisely what was called for, and I trust that foundation funds would be forthcoming to finance such a venture. I hope that in the coming years a significant minority of young historians, particularly those most concerned with the psychological aspects of historical interpretation, will be going through personal analysis under the guidance of experienced clinicians. For the others, it may be possible to work out a shorter program in consultation with the Psychoanalytic Institutes established near some of our major universities.

Nothing less, I believe, will be adequate to the needs of historical understanding in the second half of the twentieth century. I see no other approach—in the contemporary intellectual setting—that remotely matches psychoanalysis in cultivating that "feel" which has always been the particular mark of the born historian, as of the analyst. But I do not claim that such a course of training will do the job in itself. It should not be thought of as a substitute for the self-education—the gradual growth in personal awareness—which is the historian's own lonely task. Psychoanalysis can contribute mightily to this process; it cannot take over the assignment entirely. As Theodor Mommsen reminded us almost ninety years ago: "If a professor of history thinks he is able to educate historians in the same sense as classical scholars and mathematicians can be educated, he is under a dangerous and detrimental delusion. The historian . . . cannot be educated, he has to educate himself."[11]

Note

Certainly one of the earliest definitions of the "demonic" is that given by Goethe in *Dichtung und Wahrheit:*[12]

He [Goethe] thought that he discovered in Nature, animate and inanimate, with soul and without soul, something which was only manifested in contradictions, and therefore could not be grasped under one conception, still less under one word. It was not god-like, for it seemed unreasonable; not human, for it had no understanding; not devilish, for it was beneficent; not angelic, for it often showed malicious pleasure. It resembled chance, for it exhibited no consequence; it was like Providence, for it hinted at connection. Everything which limits us seemed by it to be penetrable; it seemed to sport in an arbitrary fashion with the necessary elements of our being; it contracted time and expanded space. Only in the impossible did it seem to find pleasure, and the possible it seemed to thrust from itself with contempt.

This principle, which seemed to step in between all other principles, to separate them and to unite them, I named Demonic, after the example of the ancients, and of those who had become aware of something similar. I sought to save myself before this

[11] Rectoral Address (1874) at the University of Berlin: quoted in Ernst Cassirer, *An Essay on Man* (New Haven, 1944), p. 257.
[12] *Goethe's Autobiography: Poetry and Truth,* translated by R. O. Moon (Washington, D.C., 1949), pp. 682–684.

fearful principle, by fleeing, as was my custom, behind an image. . . .

Although that Demonic element can manifest itself in all corporeal and incorporeal things, indeed even in animals expresses itself most remarkably, yet it stands especially in the most wonderful connection with man, and forms a power which, if not opposed to the moral order of the world, yet crosses it so that one may be regarded as the warp and the other as the woof.

For the phenomena which are hereby produced there are numerous names; for all philosophies and religions have endeavoured in prose and poetry to solve this riddle, and finally to settle the thing which still remains for them henceforward unassailed.

But the Demonic element appears most fearfully when it comes forward predominatingly in some man. During my life I have been able to observe several, partly near and partly at a distance. They are not always the most excellent men either as regards intelligence or talents, and they seldom recommend themselves by goodness of heart; but a tremendous power issues from them, and they exercise an incredible dominion over all creatures, indeed, even over the elements, and who can say how far such influence will extend. All united moral powers are of no avail against it; in vain all the more enlightened part of mankind make them suspect as either deceivers or deceived, the mass will be attracted by them. Seldom or never do contemporaries find their equals, and they are to be overcome by nothing but by the universe itself with which they began the struggle, and from such remarks that strange but monstrous proverb may have arisen: *Nemo contra Deum, nisi Deus ipse.*

IV.

The Sweep of the Narrative Line

THOSE OF us who advocate experiment in historical writing may quite plausibly be charged with neglecting or denigrating the central thread of the historian's tradition. When we argue for a schematic account of the past—for the establishment of precisely delineated processes or structures that will give to history a more clearly scientific frame—we may be accused of forgetting that historical prose has always consisted primarily of narrative. When we see suggestive virtue in the "meta-historical" flights of a Spengler or a Toynbee[1]—a type of writing which despite its scientific trappings is actually far out on the poetic limits of our craft—we may similarly be told that these vast speculations have little to do with the historian's main business. Whether we try to bring history closer to social science or to give greater scope to the wanderings of

[1] See particularly the concluding chapter and Appendix II, pp. 183–187 (on Toynbee), of my *Oswald Spengler: A Critical Estimate*, revised edition (New York, 1962); also Frank E. Manuel, "In Defense of Philosophical History," *The Antioch Review*, XX (Fall 1960), 331–343. Manuel and I reached our positive judgment on meta-history quite independently of each other.

its artistic fancy—in either case our knuckles are rapped. The main business, we are reminded, is narrative: that is what distinguishes the writing of history from all other intellectual pursuits. As its very name keeps recalling to our minds, history is a story. Alone of the learned disciplines, it tries to recapture how things happened. Others may abstract from reality to their heart's content, to select what particular aspect of man's experience they choose to analyze. History alone aspires to give a full *and real* account.

Hence history faces a problem confronted by no other discipline. It is all very well, my contradictors will say, to defend the meta-historians or to urge the merits of a schematic, quasi-scientific treatment. These may seem to be new and exciting pursuits. Yet there is another side to their apparent novelty and difficulty of execution. In one respect at least the more experimental types of history are easier to compose than the historical writing of tradition. For like science or art, they are *partially arbitrary* abstractions from reality. Such abstractions have never fully satisfied the historian and probably never will. A true historian yearns to grasp reality itself, to convey the nature of "becoming," to plunge, as the philosopher Bergson aspired to do, into the flux of human experience. If he is born to his craft, he will settle for nothing less.

Is this an impossible goal? Is the historian's effort to convey, through narrative, a sense of how it felt to participate in the great events of the past—is this in any sense feasible? Or is it perhaps one of those generous illusions essential to men embarked on a futile but magnificent quest? I myself am of two minds on these questions. And I think that the best way to try to answer them is to examine first what historians actually do when they undertake to write narrative prose and then to see how these narratives relate to the more experimental types of historical writing that I have discussed in the earlier essays.

I have never meant to belittle narrative history. We who have argued the merits of other historical genres have no intention of substituting a new type of writing for an old. We do not want to displace narrative history from its traditional central role: we recognize that most of the classics of history as literature are cast in the narrative mold, and that the telling of a story will continue to be an indispensable feature of our endeavor. After all, it is chronological sequence that most sharply distinguishes the writing of history from all other intellectual pursuits. What we are after, rather, is an enrichment of historical understanding; we want to find out what sort of understanding can be reached through prose that is primarily narrative and in what respects our subject matter can benefit from a more analytic or schematic type of study. At the very least, if we look once again at history's traditional storytelling function from the standpoint of twentieth-century historians with a primarily analytic emphasis, we may be able to assess with greater accuracy the scope and limitations of the narrative method.

One generalization immediately springs to mind—narrative history is far less simple a matter than it appears to be. On this, both its defenders and its detractors will agree. As the primary vehicle for historical literature through two and a half millennia of writing, the narrative has been refined and polished to a highly professional finish. Historians have developed a myriad of literary devices for gliding over what they do not adequately know or understand. With more schematic history, the gaps yawn embarrassingly wide: in narrative prose, they can be artfully concealed. Moreover, if the analytic historian makes a judgment, he is usually explicit about it: the story-teller can slip such a judgment into a highly colored adjective or a subordinate clause without alerting the reader to what he is doing. Thus most narrative history does not quite live up to its advance billing: it is neither as comprehensive nor as "objective" as it is popularly supposed to be.

Let us take a look at the typical accounts of times past and see what in fact they "cover." In most of such accounts the method is actually closer to that of the novel or the drama than the author explicitly recognizes. Just as in fiction told in the third person, we find on closer inspection that there is often a leading character whose point of view is dominant— who might as well be the "I" by whom the story is told—so in history we can detect the figure or figures through whose eyes the historian witnesses the events he describes. He may think of himself as an omniscient quasi-deity serenely viewing human affairs from an altitude of lofty detachment. In fact, he is condemned to be a mere mortal and is obliged to pick from among his cast of characters those to whom he will extend his imaginative sympathy. And these will almost of necessity be from the higher ranks—statesmen, commanding generals, or perhaps an occasional wise intimate of the great. It is hard to find a political history written from the standpoint of the ordinary voter or the account of a battle which reflects the sentiments of the suffering enlisted man. And this is not through any snobbery or hard-heartedness on the part of the historian. It is simply that the voter or the common soldier has a "worm's eye view" of the matter. He cannot possibly provide the range of vision that the historian requires in order to carry out his task.

But is even the view of the statesman or the general as comprehensive as it seems to be? Of course not—it is limited in all sorts of ways, and most obviously by locale. In devising his account, the historian finds himself obliged to proceed like a dramatist. He cannot be everywhere at once (in this respect also, he is only a mortal); he must shift his action from one place to another, as his own judgment or feel tells him how to focus his story. And these theaters or stages are once again of the loftier sort—the halls of parliament, a cabinet meeting, a staff headquarters. Concentrated thus, the account becomes detailed and specific; sometimes even snatches of dialogue find a place. Here the historian behaves almost like a participant himself, as he strives to recreate the reality and to convey the excitement of the meeting in question. Just as only a few characters enjoy the historian's inner sympathy—can have some actuality breathed into them as the author pauses for a moment to catch a glimpse of events through their eyes—while the others are relegated to the rank of what the French call mere *figurants,* so it is only on an infinitesimal minority of the vast welter of human experiences that the historian can turn his full narrative power; the rest must remain background, externally viewed, for which a lifeless summary has to suffice.

The narrative, then, proceeds on two levels: out in front, the great scenes; behind, the vast anonymity of all the rest of the living and acting and dying. It is hard to see how the historian can do otherwise. Yet what starts as a technical necessity is reinforced by personal preference and mental sloth. Where "the documents" lead, the historian follows; and if these documents are official in nature, his account becomes that much easier, for it is as guides to the major scenes that official records chiefly function. With this observation, we land right in the middle of one of the historian's most cherished illusions —the myth of the eyewitness account.

Eyewitness of what? The manuals tell us that the accounts of participants rank directly after official documents as prime "sources," since the authors are writing of events they saw with their own eyes. But how much did they actually see (leaving quite aside the question of how much they could accurately remember)? This can be only a small segment of the large events on which their word commands authority, the rare occasions on which they were both physically present and mentally alert. For most of what figures in participants' accounts, the authors are no better off than the rest of us: they know it only at second hand. I have found it a useful exercise for my students to subject to critical examination such a celebrated work by a great participant as Winston Churchill's *The Second World War*. Surely here is a series of volumes whose authoritative character no one will question. Yet when we ask how much of the war Mr. Churchill truly "saw," the answer is a very small portion indeed. Only a few fragments of his six volumes are really at firsthand—and these again are the great scenes, the set pieces which the narrative historian has always adored.

If the historian did not permit hearsay evidence, how could he possibly piece together his story? Here the parallel between history and a court of law, dear to the philosophers of our craft, is quite misleading. The historian does not really proceed in the fashion either of a judge or of an attorney. "The lawyer aims to make a case; the historian wishes to understand a situation. The evidence which convinces lawyers often fails to satisfy us; our methods seem singularly imprecise to them."[2] I had the misfortune once to be a witness in a court of law, and I recall my frustration at the judge's constantly ruling out of order the points that I regarded as most significant. "Fact is fact," he scolded me, "and hearsay is hearsay"; presumably in the judge's mind the two neither met nor overlapped. In my own experience, whether as historian or as participant, I had found no such clear line of demarcation.

Personal experience can serve as a useful check on how far the knowledge of participants—or the record of their doings—actually extends. Fabrice in *La Chartreuse de Parme* was puzzled as to whether he had or had not fought in the Battle of Waterloo. Veterans of the Second World War may recall a similar puzzlement when they found themselves unaccountably awarded battle stars for service in which they had never heard a shot fired in anger; they simply happened to be inside the conventional lines in time and space with which the higher headquarters had defined the limits of a battle. At the center of a historical phenomenon, those directly involved may have a reasonably clear idea of what is going on. On the periphery, bewilderment takes over.

And what of a mass phenomenon in which there is no identifiable center or point of direction? How is the narrative historian to tell the story of a mob action in which it is impossible to distinguish leaders from led? Even in the less amorphous case of an election, it is one thing to record the activities of the candidates, quite another to trace how the voters came to a series of individual decisions that eventually added up to the

[2] A. J. P. Taylor, *The Origins of the Second World War* (New York, 1962), p. 13.

verdict of numbers. When the election is over it all seems clear: how could we ever have doubted the outcome? But just the day before, the same electoral landscape offered nothing but confusion. It is a sobering experience to cast one's thought over the thousands of dwellings in a whole sprawling constituency and to try to determine what is going on inside each voter's mind as the moment of decision approaches. Those who have made the attempt may be justly skeptical of the confident fashion in which historians pronounce on corresponding events in the past. Similarly, anyone who has followed his own activities in the current press may well be struck with wonder at the credence which historians conventionally give to newspaper articles of an earlier day. I used to know an elderly statesman who told me that in forty years of public life he had never once read an accurate newspaper account of his own doings.

Must we despair, then, of ever producing a satisfactory story of the past? If the narrative historian's sympathetic understanding extends no farther than the front of the stage or stages he has devised, if his account blurs at the edges and shakes even at the center, is he justified in claiming to have told the tale of how things came to be as they are? Not exactly—the historian does not quite perform what he says he does. But he accomplishes something else, and this is no small feat. He locates and describes the key events—what we conventionally call the turning points of history—some of which may have been visible as such to the participants themselves, others appearing in this light only with the passage of time.

Thus the historian who prides himself on the comprehensive scope of his narrative is usually unaware of what he has actually done. He fails to see how radical a selection he has been obliged to make among the number of courses open to him, and how in this respect his situation is not so very different from that of the historian who frankly fits his material into a scheme that he has himself composed. In both cases, the writer has established his own criteria of relevance; in both cases, these criteria derive, whether consciously or by implication, from the historian's own value system. However he chooses to proceed, he—the historian—is the one who is directing the show: the events will not do it for him.

Within the limits of this radical selectivity, what the narrative historian *can* convey is the direction of change through time. He can try to chart how one human situation was gradually transformed into another. But he is unable to trace the process every step of the way. Men's activities come in an uninterrupted flow, and by the very effort to describe this flow, the historian is obliged to chop it up into segments. Such are the episodes in time and space on which he chooses to focus his attention. Here the historian pauses to take a bearing, to sketch a scene, to depict an individual character, or to mount a dramatic action. But these are merely the way stations: the crucial significance lies in the points of arrival and of departure. At those points alone can the historian find some sure footing, and it is the mark of the writer who knows his trade to have chosen them with discernment. No literary device can trace the entire trajectory of an object in motion: it can specify only the beginning and the end.

More broadly, our verbal metaphors are powerless to convey the infinite richness and inextricable connectedness of human experience. We may speak of flux, texture, dense interpenetration—all these are inadequate. Yet once again, even without finding fully satisfactory words for expressing it, the historian knows whereof he speaks. And he knows also that the greatest challenge he faces is the imperative to render in one continuous sweep of prose style both the direction of events and their simultaneous occurrence. He must keep his narrative moving in the direction he has found significant; at the same time he is obliged to take account of the multiple viewpoints on the past characteristic of the modern temper. He must find a literary method which combines narrative pace with analytic richness—which holds together change through time and the vast simultaneity of human doings.

Hence the historian's supreme technical virtuosity lies in fusing the new method of social and psychological analysis with his traditional storytelling function. If he can keep the "how" and the "why" moving steadily alongside each other—if he can shift easily back and forth from the multiple doubts and hesitations of the participants to the single certainty of the historian who knows the outcome—then he is a writer who understands his business well. The trick is to follow now one, now another, of the aspects of experience—economic innovation, psychological shock, social regrouping, as the case may be—in their parallel or interacting effects, and to pick up each in turn, shifting it to the foreground as it impinges on the major human change which the central narrative is carrying, until finally all the streams of interpretation converge. The point of convergence is, of course, of the historian's own choosing, but there are some points well chosen and others that are not. The sign that it is a good choice is when the whole broad range of the original narrative or analysis, the multiple streams that the historian has been coaxing along, come together effortlessly and as though without prior design.

Such convergences have varied widely with the differing tempers of historians and the events to which they have given central importance. Michelet preferred to work with a *tableau*—a set piece of wide dimensions that would establish pictorially in the reader's mind the end result of a long historical chain. To close his account of the Middle Ages, he chose the trial and death of Joan of Arc. This tragic fragment of history, to which our contemporary dramatists have returned again and again, as though forever dissatisfied with established answers, at Michelet's hands became the individual expression of transition from the era of religious faith to the era of national states: "This last figure of the past was also the first of the time that was beginning. In her appeared the Virgin . . . and already the Fatherland."[3] In the brief career of Joan of Lorraine—half idyl and half inferno—Michelet found the ideal vehicle to convey his own sense of historical paradox and human contradiction, and with it a view of the medieval twilight that imposed itself on his successors.

Another type of convergence may be found in the single episode that brings into final focus a long and complex development. In *To the Finland Station*, Edmund Wilson, after tracing a full century of historical study exploited to revolutionary ends—and with Michelet himself figuring as a precursor—located the moment of climax with Lenin's arrival by train in Petrograd in April 1917. The Bolshevik leader's impromptu harangue from an armored car seemed to Wilson to mark the decisive moment when revolutionary thought went over into action; after Marx's decades of laborious study and writing, his ideological heirs were at last ready to put into prac-

---

[3] *History of France*, translated by G. H. Smith (New York, 1845), II, 168. I have altered the translation.

tice what the master had taught, through identifying their own deeds with the course of history. After that decisive April evening, the writing and the acting of history would never be quite the same again.

Such a device may strike the professional historian as too much the contrivance of a belletrist who has been insufficiently disciplined in seminar. But a close scrutiny of some highly professional contemporary writing reveals that similar techniques enjoy a perfectly respectable standing. I am thinking, for example, of a biographical study of Darwin's leading American disciple, John William Draper. The supreme moment in the life of this fervent propagator of "the religion of science" comes with his trip to England in 1860 and his reading a paper to an Oxford audience riven by the controversy over *The Origin of Species*, which had been published the previous year. The scene is a familiar one to students of English thought—once again a kind of parliament hall, this time a parliament of science, where Thomas Huxley, for the Darwinians, puts the orthodox Bishop Wilberforce to rout. Yet despite countless retellings, the role of the visitor from America has remained obscure: it is only now that we realize his individual importance in delivering the paper which precipitated the crucial exchange and thereby widened the controversy beyond the narrowly scientific limits within which the Darwinians of strict observance were trying to confine it. In this consciousness of the broader issues at stake, Draper and Wilberforce saw alike:

Both men saw, or at least sensed, that the emotions would feel the impress of the new theory. It was not for them a limited-liability enterprise, but an assault, for better or worse, on the whole intellectual, emotional, and ethical structure of the European world. The theory of evolution could not be quarantined;

it must spread its contagion from one end to the other of human thought and through the whole range of final commitments within which thought operates.

And so we find that it was the lesser figure in the debate who sensed more clearly where the controversy was heading— that it would end by shaking the entire "emotional and intellectual habitat of ordinary Victorian man."[4] Here once more, by turning the prism of his vision just a few degrees, the historian has caught familiar material in a new light and elegantly located a critical convergence. And he has done something more: as our previous specimens have suggested, it is not sufficient that the writer assemble the various strands of his account into a single climactic episode; this episode itself should ideally become the point of departure for a new sweep of historical prose. Beyond the summit point of the narrative, the succeeding paragraphs and chapters may broaden the scope of the account, in ever widening circles, until the reader discovers with delight that what seemed to be no more than an artistic summation has in fact revealed unsuspected implications from which a whole new series of explanatory sequences have taken their rise.

Those of us who define our vision of history in terms of a retrospective cultural anthropology have stressed the central importance of symbols in establishing the common values of a given culture. These symbols may be of all types and degrees of specificity—religious, aesthetic, moral—yet they have in common their power to hold together heterogeneous manifestations of the human spirit whose inner connection people sel-

[4] Donald Fleming, *John William Draper and the Religion of Science* (Philadelphia, 1950), pp. 72–73.

dom express in logical form. The symbol conveys the implicit principles by which the society lives, the shared understanding of assumptions which require no formal proof..

Most characteristically such symbols are plastic. They point their message through an image or picture. And so is it also with narrative history. As Georges Sorel was one of the first to discover, most people do not understand their history in terms of careful chronology or reasoned explanation; they *see* it rather, as images of the apocalyptic battles which have changed the world. For Christians there stands the supreme drama of the crucifixion, for revolutionaries the compelling examples of 1789 and 1917, for Americans the tragic riddle of the Civil War. These are the historical myths that bind the group together: it was Sorel again who taught us that the popular understanding of history must necessarily be in terms of myth.

But what does this have to do with the narratives composed by professional historians? Surely the trained historical craftsman can and does rise above the vulgar mythology of the populace. In a purely technical sense he does—and yet in another and perhaps more profound sense he is dependent on the popular understanding for the very origin and form of his writing. I tried to show a moment ago that the crucial passages in the best narrative histories depict dramatic episodes where time sequences converge in one tense point of concentration before sweeping out once again into a new explanatory succession. These convergences are primarily pictorial—and by psychological necessity. For in his basic mental equipment the historian is no different from his untutored readers; he also must fuse his material into a summary picture in order to get an adequate grasp upon it. This is perhaps what Croce had in mind when he coined his baffling formula of a "lightning

flash" of understanding; what seemed an opaque way of describing a process of logical explanation suddenly becomes clear
if we apply it to the pictorial creations of the narrative historian,
a role in which Croce could also on occasion turn in a distinguished performance.

The true relationship between expert history and popular
myth is neither as simple as it would be if the professionals
merely set mythology straight, nor as discouraging as if trained
historians did nothing more than embrace the popular belief.
The real relation between the two is one of constant interaction.
As Vico discovered two and a half centuries ago, historical
myths have a "public ground of truth" which needs only to
be "cleaned, pieced together, and restored." The historian cannot even begin to devise his account until he knows what this
mythology is; unless he reckons with his readers' prior preparation, unless he starts from their half-conscious assumptions
about their own past, there is not the remotest chance that he
will be listened to. He may eventually choose to jar them into
a new understanding; but he has to begin with what is already
a familiar feature of their mental landscape.

Historians, like other people, first learned their history as
children, and if they do not retain a child's curiosity and wonder about the past, they will never be able to communicate
their subsequent understanding. As we saw much earlier, this
popular and easily accessible character of historical prose is
something that it is vital for us to preserve at a time when an
increasing professionalism is closing in upon us. The historian
originally takes his decisive events where he finds them—in the
sense common to the culture in which he grew up. Indeed,
some of his predecessors have been the first architects of the
popular mythology. A few historical events shape themselves in

the public mind without apparent effort: appropriate labels are almost immediately found, and the canon of episodes worth remembering is established very early; the French Revolution and our own Civil War are cases in point. Most of the time, however, the conventional delimiting of events proceeds slowly, and historians may wrangle for generations until some one of them—like Oscar Handlin with the phenomenon of immigration—finally affixes the stamp that wins general favor.

In this fashion the historian both echoes and rectifies popular belief. Sometimes he merely deepens the common understanding of a crucial turning point; at other times he argues his public into accepting a new one. Or—as in the case of the fall of France in 1940—he may show them that a familiar dramatic sequence needs to be understood in a new sense. The original view of the French military defeat—that it was the direct result of political and social "decay"—telescoped into a simple cause and effect relationship a series of events whose interlockings were much less direct. On closer study, we have concluded that the military disaster had little connection with a loss of confidence in parliamentary government; it can mostly be ascribed to the incompetence of the French generals. Its relationship to the polemics against democracy that had marked the preceding decade was parallel and catalytic; by shattering the public values by which the French lived, the military defeat precipitated out of a latent mood of ideological questioning a full-scale counterrevolution.

I sometimes suspect that in the course of correcting the old myths the historians themselves create new ones. I am thinking, for example, of the amount of speculation that has surrounded Hitler's meeting with a group of Rhine-Ruhr industrialists at the house of the banker Schroeder in early January 1933. Here

we have a dramatic gathering that was supposed to be secret
and hence was unknown to the general public until after the
fall of the Third Reich. It was only then that historians found
evidence of a tacit bargain which enabled Hitler to reach the
chancellorship less than a month later: the businessmen under-
took to pay the Nazis' debts; the Nazi leader for his part gave
assurances that he would not touch the basic capitalist structure
of the German economy.[5] I think that this assessment of the
situation in early 1933 is substantially correct: some such understanding was an essential preliminary to the conservatives'
acceptance of Hitler as chancellor. But I question whether a
single meeting had the crucial significance which historians
have subsequently ascribed to it; I think that the reassurance
extended to the business classes was a more amorphous matter
—that it did not go beyond hints and symptomatic gestures.

In cases like these, the historian's great temptation is to make
a single episode bear too much explanatory weight. He is carried away by the power of his own narration, succumbing himself to the aesthetic preferences of his audience. Yet even in
the more doubtful cases, he is also showing them something
they did not know before. By casting his view forward from the
"pact" of January 1933, the historian lets his readers in on the
sequels and the paradoxes of the outcome. Which partner to
the bargain was fooling which? Did anyone present have the
slightest suspicion where an agreement so casually arrived at
would lead—that it would end twelve years later in the fiery
ruins of that chancellery which Hitler was now in such a hurry
to enter? Or perhaps did one or two of the more sensitive

[5] George W. F. Hallgarten, "Adolf Hitler and German Heavy Indus-
try, 1931–1933," *The Journal of Economic History*, XII (Summer 1952),
222–246.

present unconsciously long for some such *Götterdämmerung?*
The historian's most intoxicating task is to demonstrate the
irony of historical action, the day of dupes repeated in infinite
succession until only the end of humanity itself can determine
who has the last laugh. Some historical figures achieve what
they set out to do; other accomplish the opposite; perhaps the
most characteristic attain against their announced intention the
things that at a deeper level they wanted all along. And what
better way for the historian to suggest this cosmic irony than
through the constant reworking of the great myth scenes in our
common past?

Most of the examples I have presented are from political and
military history. And this for good reason. The narrative historian shares with his readers the conviction that politics and
war should carry the central narrative thread. This may seem
a depressingly old-fashioned conclusion from someone who has
undertaken to reconnoiter the frontier posts in contemporary
historical writing. Have two centuries of experiment with the
histories of all the other products of man's spirit ended only in
a return to parliaments and battles?

I am far from suggesting that this is all. But I think that the
more sophisticated historians—and readers—need to be reminded that here once more the common understanding is
basic to what they do. The public forms its notion of current
history by what it reads in the newspapers; wars and threats of
war predominate. In these the ordinary reader discerns the narrative motion within his society that seems to establish the
temporal framework for its routine activities. And the historian
also, if he wants to convey how the members of that society
themselves conceived the public dimension of their lives, is

obliged to proceed likewise. The sort of analytic history that deals in statistical aggregates—economic, demographic, and the like—cannot possibly give the sense of personal immediacy inherent in the doings of generals and statesmen. Indeed, one of the great problems of analytic history is to acquire something of this face-to-face character; hence the importance of community studies in bringing the more repetitive of men's activities into human scale.

Thus the new analytic type of history can learn from the traditional narrative as well as enrich the latter with its unorthodox techniques and insights. The narrative approach can give human warmth and actuality to economic and social generalization; analytic tools of investigation can aid in the never-ending process of correcting the popular notion of history's mythical moments—by suggesting where the activities of generals and statesmen had a truly decisive effect and where they were merely episodic or anecdotal. If we historians can do both of these things at the same time—if we can refresh the old narrative with unsuspected vistas of understanding, while losing nothing of its motion and vitality—then we shall indeed have inaugurated a new era in historical studies. To make a sharp separation between narrative and analytic method is not at all what we are after; it is rather to fuse the two in a brighter and clearer illumination of the past.

Both partake of history's twin character as art and as science. The artistic aspects of the narrative are patent: they have been the main burden of the present essay. But one feature of its scientific character may not have emerged so explicitly. To narrate is also to predict. Here once again the very nature of the historian's mental equipment dictates what he does, however much his conscious intention may deny it. The historian conventionally refuses to make predictions; he says this is not his business and leaves it to the more schematic social sciences. But in fact he *implies* predictions all the time. He cannot stop his prose in midstream.

The historian . . . is bound to generalize; and, in so doing, he provides general guides for future action which, though not specific predictions, are both valid and useful. But he cannot predict specific events, because the specific is unique and because the element of accident enters into it. This distinction, which worries philosophers, is perfectly clear to the ordinary man. If two or three children in a school develop measles, you will conclude that the epidemic will spread; and this prediction, if you care to call it such, is based on a generalization from past experience, and is a valid and useful guide to action. But you cannot make the specific prediction that Charles or Mary will catch measles.[6]

The historian will not call the shots. Yet like other types of scientists he will delimit what is possible, what is probable, and what is almost certain. Most of the time he will do it by indirection, by simply organizing his statement of past events so that they move toward other events that lie in the future. This we call retrospective prediction. For the subsequent series of events does not really lie in the future—*the historian's* future—but merely in the future of the participants in the initial series. Such predictions are by definition accurate: here we recall the historian's privileged position of knowing the outcome. But what happens when the chain of retrospection comes to an end? What is the historian to do when he reaches his own present— when he loses his special knowledge and becomes a blind participant like anyone else, peering into the future as best he may?

[6] Edward Hallett Carr, *What Is History?* (New York, 1961), pp. 87–88.

Does he give up the predictive character of his thought? Does he radically recast the structure of his narrative sentences so as to shut off their built-in motion toward the future? I do not think he does so, and I do not think he ought to do so. He can and does continue just as before. He continues to project his line of analysis into a future that is now actually, rather than merely by literary convention, unknown to him. All this will become amply apparent, I think, when we turn now to examine the perils and the joys of writing the history of our own time.

V.

Is Contemporary History Real History?

WHEN I was a student, I had the strong impression that the writing and teaching of contemporary history were not quite respectable. It was rumored that in Europe a full century had to pass before a subject was considered ripe for historical treatment, and that the whole period since the French Revolution fell into the suspect category of the contemporary. Even in my own country, I noticed, the college courses which were labeled "since" a given date and hence presumably went right to the present, in fact stopped or petered out at least a decade before the year in which they were given. There always yawned a gap, of varying dimensions, between the date at which the formal study of history stopped and the onset of the individual age of reason when I had begun to read the current news with understanding. So far as I can tell, something of this situation still persists. I have found my students' knowledge at its vaguest on the period of their own childhood: Hitler today is scarcely more real than Attila the Hun. Since the recent past seems to the young just as alien as the remote past, I have concluded that there is no good reason for not treating it as equally historical, and I have labored to eliminate the gap of ignorance that so troubled my student years by bringing my own lectures abreast of the morning newspapers.

Yet still the doubts of an earlier day have never ceased bothering me. To many—perhaps to most—of my fellow historians the history of one's own time is not "real" history. It suffers from certain irremediable insufficiencies that make it less than history—current events, perhaps, or even political science, but not history in the usual meaning of the term. These presumed insufficiencies—of documentation, of perspective, and of detachment or "objectivity"—need to be examined with some care if I am to convince myself and others that all this time I have not been embarked on a fool's errand.

The most familiar charge leveled against contemporary history is that it cannot be written since we do not yet have "the documents." It would be foolish to deny the force of this reproach. The Soviet archives are closed to scholars and seem likely to remain so; how many other important repositories are under seal I would not care to estimate. No one will quarrel with the assertion that the historian who tries to write about the mid-twentieth century is laboring under handicaps he would not suffer if he were dealing with an earlier period.

I do not think, however, that this handicap is as great as it is commonly supposed to be. The stress on documentary insufficiency derives from a corresponding overestimation of the value of documents themselves—a point that I have repeatedly touched on earlier in these essays and that should now be explained more fully. Obviously it is impossible to write most types of history without documentation to go on. But we should not ask too much of written sources. "No document," E. H. Carr reminds us, "can tell us more than what the author of the document thought—what he thought had happened, what he thought ought to happen or would happen, or perhaps only what he wanted others to think he thought, or even only what he himself thought he thought."[1]

The cult of documents, like so much else in historical writing, can itself be explained historically. It goes back to the beginnings of systematic scholarship, when Catholic and Protestant divines tried to demolish each other's arguments by assailing the validity of old canonical texts, or discovering new ones, and it was reinforced in the first half of the nineteenth century when Leopold von Ranke based his seminar training on the systematic exploitation of documentary materials. Ranke's favorite sources were the *relazioni* of Venetian ambassadors—the wide-ranging reports of cool, experienced diplomats, surveying the international scene with the poise and skepticism befitting the representatives of a small state whose disproportionate influence reflected a cultivated finesse in manipulating the European balance of power. Such an attitude suited the temperament of a young historian sensitive to nuances of policy and character. Or perhaps the long-deceased Venetian ambassadors molded the historian's mind to conform to their own. *"Der Stoff brachte die Form mit sich"*—"the material imposed the form" of his history—Ranke unguardedly remarked, thereby admitting that he was allowing his sources to ride *him* rather than guiding *them* with a firm hand. Whatever the process, in the end there came to be a close fit between the historian and the materials with which he was working.

From this elective affinity derived a number of consequences of great importance to subsequent historical scholarship. First

[1] *What Is History?* (New York, 1961), p. 16.

there was the tendency we have already observed to view events with the eyes of a statesman, simply taking for granted the great-power system and the diplomatic status quo. Along with it went the further assumption that war and diplomacy were the historian's main business—what Ranke called the primacy of foreign policy—which even in our own country won general acceptance, thereby provoking in reaction the contemporary tendency to begin with internal policy and to deal with foreign affairs as the outward reflection of internal struggles. Still more, the tidy and finite character of diplomatic dispatches persuaded historians that other types of documentation were equally manageable. The less reflective jumped to the conclusion that in every field of historical investigation there existed a body of documents as clearly delimited as these; they forgot that on certain subjects—as for administrative history—the documentation might be overwhelming in its mass and heterogeneity, while elsewhere it might be almost nonexistent. Above all, the cult of documents tended to discourage direct observation: diplomacy, as a closed and semi-secret preserve, was almost the last place where the historian would have an opportunity to do his own field work. Here the Second World War had a most fortunate by-product. Quite a number of historians, both British and American, found themselves in foreign service, and the directness and reality of their writing on diplomatic history gained immeasurably by this wartime experience.

Even for past centuries, then, the historian's conventional assumption that there is such a thing as "the documents," readily identifiable and existing in finite quantity, breaks down on closer inspection. For our own era, it becomes a near absurdity. Since the invention of the typewriter and of the more modern and flashy forms of reproducing devices, the amount of administrative paper in circulation—of typed or dittoed or multilithed material that can lay claim to the dignity of official documentation—has passed all human bounds. At the other end of the scale, the habitual use of the long-distance telephone and the practice of airplane travel have effected an equally drastic reduction: when the great chat with each other over the transatlantic wire or go long journeys for a brief personal encounter, many of their most important exchanges may never be recorded. Gone are the days when a diplomat sitting at some distant post—conscious that he might not receive instructions for weeks or see his chief for years, and that his dispatches would necessarily be read under circumstances far different from those in which they were composed—was obliged to write with something of the historian's serenity and detachment. Today we have only the urgent message—or silence in the record. The result is a vast unevenness in what the historian has to work on, an *embarras de richesse* combined with and canceled out by the most distressing lacunae. The neat coverage of eighteenth- and nineteenth-century documentation has quite vanished. In some respects, the historian of today is in the happiest situation his breed has ever enjoyed. (Yet in this too-ample pasture the honest admit that they are reduced to selective grazing.) Elsewhere, the contemporary historian may be no better off than the medievalist struggling with an almost total documentary gap.

Let us agree, then—cheerfully rather than in despair—that for the mid-twentieth century there will never come a time when "the documents" are available. Yet this history must be written; the public demands it and has a right to demand it. If we do not do the job, others less qualified will undertake it for us. Nor is the idea of writing the history of one's own time as

unconventional as certain of the manuals make it appear. Historians have always done it, even in the nineteenth century
when the notion of its disreputability was first established. Still
more, many of the works that we honor as the classics of our
craft fall into this category. I shall have occasion to comment
on some of them later on. Of course, their authors wrote without adequate documentation; of course, their conclusions have
been substantially corrected by subsequent scholarship. But
these works still stand—at the very least as literature and as
monuments of human observation.

Perhaps that is all that the writing of contemporary history
can accomplish. Yet it is already a great deal. Short on documents, certain to be superseded in detail, the historian of his
own time can still produce a work of art which will illuminate
for posterity the perceptions and the illusions of his contemporaries. That this is no mean feat will become amply apparent
when we turn to the deeper and more troubling questions of
perspective and objectivity.

By now nearly all of us have accepted Croce's dictum that
the writing of history necessarily changes with the standpoint
of the historian, that *all* history is contemporary in the sense
that its presentation reflects the circumstances and attitudes of
those who write it. Each generation writes history anew. There
is no such thing as a "definitive" work of historical scholarship.
Or, more precisely, if there are a few books whose authority
has gone unquestioned for more than a generation, it is because
the events with which they deal have been temporarily removed
from current controversy, and historians have heard no urgent
call to take a new look at them.

From this standpoint, the second major count against contemporary history—that is, "contemporary" in the usual sense of the term—the charge that we do not as yet have sufficient perspective upon it, simply falls to the ground. It is true that some minimum of time (perhaps only a matter of months) must elapse before we consciously begin to sort out the great events from the small. But this process of evaluation has actually been taking place in our minds all along. (We knew at the time that the crisis over Cuba in the spring of 1961 was a big event; what we did not know was that it would be dwarfed by a greater Cuban crisis a year and a half later.) There is no set point at which contemporary polemics cease and historical judgment takes over; the two proceed simultaneously, in the remote past as in the present.

In any ultimate sense, the best (or the worst) that the passage of time can do to contemporary events is to make them appear smaller, to reduce their image in the mirror of eternity. But this fate may not befall them right away; a number of generations or even centuries may go by before historical minutiae that once seemed of supreme importance fall into irrelevancy. When I was a student, we pursued the history of the French Revolution in meticulous detail; we were fully informed about all the shifts of party allegiance and ideological statement that punctuated the 1790's. Today, a generation later, these matters tend to be dealt with in a more summary fashion. The reason, I think, is again a change in collective experience. My student years were the 1930's—an era of passionate ideological involvement, the decade that in retrospect looks like the Indian summer of ideology itself before the very concept was swallowed up in the amorphous blandness of contemporary political exchange. Nowadays religion or social status may strike the students as more pressing matters for his-

torical investigation, and old controversies that to my college
generation seemed trivial and stale—like the points at issue
between Luther and Calvin—may unexpectedly take on a
burning urgency.

More closely regarded, then, the matter of historical perspective begins to blend with the third question and the most misunderstood of all, that of detachment or objectivity. To cite
once more my student experience, I remember that at one time
I really believed that the writer or teacher of history could and
should attain to a sublime detachment. As the French put it,
he should be above the *mêlée* of human events, delivering with
sovereign confidence the "verdict of posterity." Since then an
intense exposure to the ideas of Benedetto Croce has cured me
of such notions: I have learned that the result of the historian's
efforts to be detached has usually been the very opposite of
what anyone would call great history. It has been bloodless
history, with no clear focus, arising from antiquarian curiosity
rather than from deep personal concern, and shot through with
metaphysical and moral assumptions that are all the more
insidious for being artfully concealed.

This does not mean that I—and others like me—have
learned from Croce to write partisan history with a good conscience. Far from it: we detest mere polemic, and we certainly
know how to distinguish between fine historical writing and
writing designed to serve a cause. We recognize that historians
have been right in striving for serenity and the world-embracing
view. But we understand this aspiration in rather a different
sense from the way in which it used to be taught to us. What
we have learned from Croce and his like is that "objectivity" is
to be valued only if it is hard-won—only if it is the end result
of a desperate *and conscious* battle to rise above partisan pas-

sion. The man who does not feel issues deeply cannot write great history about them. Unaware of his own prejudices, he cannot bring them to full consciousness and thus transcend them, nor will his prose be infused with that quality of tension and excitement which comes from strong emotion just barely held under control. Only after he has mastered his own limitations can the historian begin to make constructive use of them. "Man's capacity to rise above his social and historical situation seems to be conditioned by the sensitivity with which he recognizes the extent of his involvement in it."[2] The origin of true historical curiosity, as we have just seen, is a sense of relevance for one's own time; and the criteria of such relevance derive from a passionate attachment to one's own moral and aesthetic values. With the gradual unfolding of knowledge, this passion is finally sublimated into something that can claim the dignity of historical judgment.

The same considerations apply to another and still more troubling aspect of the objectivity question—the matter of moral judgments. Acton, we recall, reproached Ranke for failing to condemn the crimes of the great historical personalities of times gone by. Yet Acton himself fell into the opposite error by scattering praise and blame wholesale throughout the centuries. Both, I think, misunderstood the real point; the real question was one of historical imagination, in which both Ranke and Acton were in their different ways equally defective. The former—as a sheltered scholar knowing nothing of war and violence—could not feel with sufficient intensity the sufferings of the victims whose execution he narrated so coolly. (I recall the shock I experienced when I suddenly realized during a tranquil reading of his *History of the Popes* that the saintly

[2] *Ibid.,* p. 54.

Counter-Reformation pontiff whose ecclesiastical house clean-
ing Ranke was implicitly endorsing was actually having heretics
burned at the stake!) Acton, in contrast, had little understanding for the agonizing dilemmas of statesmanship in eras when
cruelty was taken for granted and when killing might be the
only way to avoid being killed oneself. I do not think we have
to make a choice between these eminent examples; we are not
obliged either to declare our moral indifference or to hand out
moral judgments right and left. If we simply do our job *as
historians* with both conscientiousness and imagination, the
ethical issues will emerge clearly enough. Herbert Butterfield
puts it admirably:

The truth is that . . . we need no help from the historian to
bring us to the recognition of the criminality of religious persecution or wholesale massacre or the modern concentration camp or
the repression of dissident opinions. And those who do not recog-
nise that the killing and torturing of human beings is barbarity
will hardly be brought to that realisation by any labels and nick-
names that historians may attach to these things. There is one
way in which the historian may reinforce the initial moral judgment and thereby assist the cause of morality in general; and that
way lies directly within his province, for it entails merely describing, say, the massacre or the persecution, laying it out in
concrete detail, and giving the specification of what it means in
actuality. It is possible to say that one of the causes of moral indifference is precisely the failure to realise in an objective manner
and make vivid to oneself the terrible nature of crime and suffering; but those who are unmoved by the historical description will
not be stirred by any pontifical commentary that may be super-
added.[3]

[3] *History and Human Relations* (London, 1951), pp. 122–123.

Once more, the question of objectivity—of detachment—of moral judgment—proves to be no different whether it be the remote past or the recent present with which the historian is concerned. In the classic contrast between Ranke and Acton, the incompatibility of view remained the same both in their scholarly researches and in their comments on contemporary events. The specific point at issue was the Papacy in early modern times. But when the German historian wrote about the great powers of his own day, he endorsed the status quo with as much complacency as in swallowing the crimes of an earlier age, and when the English Catholic layman reported on the Vatican Council of 1870, he denounced the machinations of the Papal lobby with the same vigor with which he had exposed the cruelties of the Inquisition. For contemporary history and for history in the more conventional sense, the criteria and the limits of "objectivity" finally sift out as much alike. The historian can do no better than write with all honesty in the perspective his own irreducible values set for him. A conservative cannot help writing as a conservative, and a radical as a radical, and they should not feel obliged to apologize for so doing.

In both cases, the qualities of great history will emerge of themselves, whatever the specific ideological commitment of the author. I much prefer to read a book well done, but with whose assumptions I disagree, than a work based on values similar to mine which is technically or philosophically sloppy. Similarly, I think all great history has a built-in ambivalence. The historian adheres to his own ideological commitments—but another part of him understands and sympathizes with those of the enemy. The Protestant Ranke made a better case for the Popes than the Catholic Acton, and Francis Parkman, although he was convinced that the triumph of the British over the

French in North America was a good thing, could not help writing of Montcalm's death with admiration and sorrow. Here again the sublimation of the cruder passions has been at work: the historian's saving ambivalence has helped him to get beyond mere journalism or partisan polemic. The undercurrent of strong emotion remains: the urgency is still there. But through the sustained application of thought, what began as noisy controversy—whether in present or in past—has been almost miraculously transmuted into history.

"Thucydides, an Athenian, wrote the history of the war between the Peloponnesians and the Athenians, beginning at the moment that it broke out, and believing that it would be a great war, and more worthy of relation than any that had preceded it." Such is the opening sentence of the first and the most famous of contemporary histories. Two millennia later Thucydides' Italian emulator, Francesco Guicciardini, started his history on a similar note. "I have decided," he tells us, "to write down the things that happened within our memory in Italy, ever since French arms, called in by our own princes, began . . . to trouble the country." Not since the time of the Roman Empire, the historian explains, "had Italy ever enjoyed such prosperity nor experienced so desirable a state of affairs as that in which it reposed so securely in the year of our lord 1490."[4] Then came the death of Lorenzo de'Medici and the French invasions—and a generation later Italian liberty was no more.

The tone is arrestingly alike. Both Thucydides and Guicciardini had lived through the events they described; both had

Storia d'Italia, Book I.

recognized the catastrophic character of these events while they were still going on and had felt an overwhelming compulsion to explain this significance to their contemporaries while the memory was fresh in people's minds. The defeat of Athens by Sparta was for Thucydides—as it is for us—the decisive turning point in Hellenic history. For Guicciardini the French invasions, by upsetting the delicate Italian political balance, relentlessly sapped Italy's European cultural hegemony—and here once again the researches of subsequent scholars have not altered the contemporary judgment. Both Thucydides and Guicciardini combined literary distinction with an astonishingly accurate sense of the importance of their subject matter. By general assent, their creations rank as *great* contemporary history—great in theme as in execution. And the historians themselves were well aware of the extent of their own achievement; they were possessed and borne aloft by the majesty of their theme. It is worth pausing a moment over these two men to see whether from their example we can derive some clearer idea of the criteria of great contemporary history through twenty-five hundred years of historical literature.

Neither Thucydides nor Guicciardini was merely an observer. Both had been involved in responsible positions in the events they described, and both had experienced the bitterness of defeat and disgrace. Thucydides had served as an Athenian general in the early part of the Peloponnesian War; Guicciardini was a diplomat and a member of the Florentine oligarchy which had only grudgingly accepted the return of the Medici under foreign protection. Indeed both were by nature and origin traditionalist oligarchs, with a distrust of the tyrannies and popular commotions that dominated their times. Hence their sense of defeat was threefold: their personal disappoint-

ment was compounded by grief at the humiliation of their city
and their own social class.

They wrote their histories, then, with a serenity born of
despair. Retired from active participation, without hope for
the future, they felt the call to explain to their contemporaries
how these great disappointments had come to pass. The result
was a special kind of detachment, a recognition that the fault
did not all lie on one side: the incompetence of the historian's
own party had contributed to the outcome. Thucydides was
sufficiently honest to concede the Spartans' military excellence
and to expose unsparingly the Athenian fecklessness which
had led to disaster at the Siege of Syracuse; Guicciardini
finally settled for Medicean rule as the best guarantee of "good
order" after Italians of his own type had demonstrated their
political incapacity. Once more we find that the historian's
personal ambivalence is central to his account: the wrong side
has won, but the defeated, in seeking the explanation for their
own misfortunes, cannot help recognizing the ways in which
the victors proved their moral and technical superiors.

As we move down to the nineteenth century, we discover a
corresponding succession of the politically or ideologically dis-
appointed who find themselves driven by inner necessity to
write the history of their own time. In France the roster of
these *hommes politiques manqués* is particularly distinguished:
Guizot, Tocqueville, Thiers are among them. In one or two
cases, the experience of public eclipse proves only temporary:
after two decades of opposition, the old liberal Thiers is tri-
umphantly vindicated by the defeat of Napoleon III in 1870.
At other times, as with Tocqueville, the disappointment is
permanent, and life closes on a note of deep foreboding: the
European herald of American democracy does not live to see

the fall of tyranny in his own country. Yet the undercurrent of sentiment remains constant. These men know public events at firsthand; they have staked their all on politics and lost. And with this loss they have attained to an understanding that would not have been theirs had they celebrated a series of victories. With all men who have played a leading role in great events, the temptation to personal apologia may at any time become overpowering. But strange as it may sound, this temptation is the more insidious when the public figure in question does not have a failure to explain away. For here "history" does the job for him—the events themselves prove him right—and he is not obliged to make the same effort of understanding or to give his vanquished enemies their due. I doubt if De Gaulle would have written so impressive a set of memoirs if he had composed them in the flush of triumph in 1945 or in the euphoria of vindication after 1958 rather than in the lean years when all his hopes seemed in ruins.

Not all great contemporary history need sound this note of elegy. Nor does it have to be written by someone who has had a direct contact with large events. I think of these merely as a kind of optimum stance toward the material. But the tone of immediacy and urgency that characterizes all major historical writing has to come from somewhere. If it does not derive from close personal experience, then there must be a vicarious human encounter that performs the same emotional function.

If we trace the biographies of those who have chosen to be historians, we almost invariably come across an early experience that made a radical change in the individual's sense of the world around him—the shock of altered circumstance that compelled him to ask the question why. A family move to a new and exciting scene, the unexpected arrival of an exotic personality, the brutal discovery of status or class difference, the awakening of religious doubt—any one of these may give the decisive push. In my own case, a trip to France at the age of eight shattered my childhood securities. A fragile American illusion of tidy protectedness collapsed before the revelation of cruelty new and old, as the still-fresh trenches of the First World War and the horror of the forts around Verdun blended in my mind with the gray, threatening monuments of the Middle Ages, the gloomy mass of the Mont-Saint-Michel enveloped in interminable rain, the dungeons, the torture chambers, the burning of Joan of Arc, who, so far as a child from across the Atlantic could tell, had never done harm to anyone.

So this child, like all the other thousands of children before him whom history had caught in its meshes, would not rest until he had begun to inquire how such things could have been. Historical vocations usually come early, although they may not be recognized at the start for what they are. Once the imagination has been stirred, the tormenting questions may lie dormant for years until one day a lifetime commitment declares itself without apparent preparation.

I remember a historian of the starchier professorial type once declaring that it was a waste of time to teach history in school because the boys and girls would get it all wrong and would have to relearn it when they reached college. All they would retain would be some unconnected personal anecdotes and hero stories. I can scarcely imagine a judgment more mistaken. It is not a question of getting things "right"—not even the most learned historian will succeed in doing *that* in any ultimate meaning of the term. The real point is to stir the youthful imagination. And for this purpose anything will serve, no matter how suspect it may be from the standpoint of strict historical accuracy. With the very young we teachers should discard our professional fastidiousness. If the historical vision is caught in childhood, the corrections can be applied later on. But if we hobble the child's first flights of fancy, this vision may be blotted out or never appear at all.

It is notorious that Sir Walter Scott was an inaccurate historical novelist. If there ever was an imaginative writer of repute who "got things all wrong," it was he. Yet his novels of chivalry and "derring-do" (even his vocabulary was phoney) cradled the fancy of generations of future historians. When we inquire into the boyhood of leading historical writers of the nineteenth century, it is instructive to find how often Sir Walter is at the start of things. In Ranke's case, the Waverley novels lit a bonfire that blazed on for eighty years. Today there must be other historical romances—doubtless much better "researched" than were Scott's—which are kindling the same wild flame. And a teacher of history would be greatly in error if he should inadvertently put it out.

The Greek stories of gods and heroes, the legends of King Arthur, the battles of our own Civil War—the games of running and hiding that children play in open fields or city streets —simply a chance occurrence may provide the decisive impulse to reflection. It matters little, so long as the historical imagination awakens. This, we have seen, is true of all history, not merely of the history of our own time. But in the context of the first decisive questions, contemporary history plays a crucial part. In the triad formed by the present instant, the recent past, and the remote experience of our ancestors, it is the second that links the other two. It is the one step back that enables the imagination to take the great leap to what is almost totally strange. In my own case, if I had not witnessed the blasted relics of the slaughter that had been raging when I was born, my tortured fancy might not have jumped so early to the riddle of medieval cruelty.

Whether child or adult, whether amateur lover of historical literature or professional scholar forever at his task of scrupulous documentation, the historian is obliged to reckon with his own time. He cannot escape it: its pressures are all around him. And if his trade has more than antiquarian meaning for him, he will feel impelled to comment on the recent past. For the same dilemmas of personal loyalty and ideal allegiance, of inborn ruthlessness and good will toward men, which have troubled his mind in his study of remote ages will force themselves upon him when he rests his weary eyes for a moment on the circumstances in which he is actually living. Marc Bloch the medievalist was inspired by his experience in 1940 as a staff officer of the reserve to write a little study of the fall of France. And the power of his account—the most convincing analysis of that great defeat I have ever read—derives precisely from the fact that the tragedy is seen through the eyes of a man who has traced with affectionate attention more than a millennium of his country's history and whose unutterable sorrow can be glimpsed behind every balanced phrase and reasoned historical judgment.[5]

In Europe it is not uncommon for historians to practice two specialties, an early, strictly professional field and the history of their own time. In the United States a mistaken overemphasis on academic rigor has led the average scholar to confine his efforts to a single area of historical knowledge. Most spe-

[5] *Strange Defeat,* translated by Gerard Hopkins (London, 1949).

cialists, protesting their lack of professional qualifications, shun the writing of contemporary history. But in so doing they leave the field to others who are still less qualified. Indeed, the specialist on some remote area of man's experience, like Bloch, may have a particular aptitude for the comparative understanding of the almost-yesterday, an understanding that may long lie unsuspected until the accident of personal involvement suddenly brings it to conscious expression.

Somebody must interpret our era to our contemporaries. Somebody must stake out the broad lines of social change and cultural restatement, and he must not be afraid to make predictions or chagrined at being occasionally caught out on a limb. There was a time when universally minded social thinkers performed this function, when the fathers of sociology, from Montesquieu through Marx to Weber, freely speculated on where their age was heading. Today, the sociologists, like the historians, have grown cautious. The chair of speculative social thought is nearly everywhere without an occupant. Historians have peculiar qualifications to fill it, and they are already beginning to do so. For the historian who sees no incompatibility between his different roles—who is at least as much an artist as he is a social scientist—is uniquely equipped to lead others toward the imaginative fusion of these attributes, and thereby to illuminate the era in which we live.

Lightning Source UK Ltd.
Milton Keynes UK
UKHW01f2136110618
324066UK00002B/503/P